English in Focus

Series Editors: J. P. B. ALLEN and H. G. WIDDOWSON
Advisory Editor: RONALD MACKIN

ENGLISH IN FOCUS

English in Mechanical Engineering

ERIC H. GLENDINNING

TEACHER'S EDITION

OXFORD UNIVERSITY PRESS

Oxford University Press, Walton Street, Oxford OX2 6DP

OXFORD LONDON GLASGOW
NEW YORK TORONTO MELBOURNE WELLINGTON
KUALA LUMPUR SINGAPORE JAKARTA HONG KONG TOKYO
DELHI BOMBAY CALCUTTA MADRAS KARACHI
IBADAN NAIROBI DAR ES SALAAM CAPE TOWN

ISBN 019 437512 9   (Student's Edition)
ISBN 019 437501 3   (Teacher's Edition)

PRINTED AND BOUND IN ENGLAND BY
HAZELL WATSON AND VINEY LTD
AYLESBURY, BUCKS

Contents

Unit 3   Force

Unit 4   Friction

Editors' Preface

The aim of the *English in Focus* series is to develop in students who are entering higher education an ability to handle the kind of written English that they will be concerned with as an integral part of their specialist subject. The approach is one which recognizes that learning a language is not merely a matter of learning sentence patterns and vocabulary but must also involve an understanding of how people use these linguistic forms in order to communicate. Our purpose is to make students aware of the way English is used in actual written communication, and thereby to help them develop techniques of reading and to provide them with a guide for their own writing.

The books in this series are based on the belief that intermediate and advanced students who are studying English as a necessary part of their specialist studies need a distinctive type of textbook: one which reflects the nature of the learning problems encountered at this stage, and which presents the language as an aspect of the subject they are studying. We feel that a textbook directed at students at this level should attempt to do more than simply repeat the formulas in elementary language teaching material. Most courses of English concentrate on teaching the language system and fail to show how this system is used in communication. As a result, students may know about such formal items as affirmative sentences or modal verbs, but not know how these items are put to use in the making of different kinds of statements and in the production of continuous pieces of discourse.

The principal purpose of the *English in Focus* series is not to teach more grammar, but to show students how to use the grammar they already know. In writing these books two basic assumptions have been made. Firstly, it is assumed that the students have had a good deal of instruction in grammar and that they have a considerable dormant competence in English. The books are directed at activating this competence, and extending it, by leading the student to relate his previously acquired linguistic knowledge to meaningful realizations of the language system in passages of immediate relevance to his specialist studies. Secondly, it is assumed that students already have a basic knowledge of their specialist subject. The aim is not to teach subject-matter but to develop in the reader an understanding of how this subject-matter is expressed through English. It should be emphasized that these books are not designed to teach either language in isolation or subject-matter in isolation but the manner in which both combine in meaningful communication. Our belief is that by relating content and expression in this way, the subject-matter takes on a new interest and the linguistic difficulties are reduced.

In order to ensure the natural communicative function of language, grading is by *focus* rather than by *exclusion*. Since it is assumed that the readers of these books already have a fairly wide knowledge of English grammar, and also have access to a standard dictionary and other reference books, the authors have been able to avoid an unnatural step-by-step presentation of grammatical patterns and vocabulary, and instead aim to show how a fluent writer uses the whole resources of the language in performing various acts of communication. At the same time, care has been taken not to overload the student with new material and complex structures have been avoided except where they are necessary in maintaining a natural use of language. We believe that the books in the series will prepare the student to cope with greater linguistic complexity by developing in him a reading strategy which he can bring to bear on the material in the textbooks he has to read.

In the exercises an attempt has been made to avoid the more mechanical types of drill. The users of these books will be people whose minds are directed towards rational thought and problem-solving and the exercises have been designed to take this fact into account. Wherever possible, exercises are used which require the sort of mental activity which students would naturally be engaged in as part of their specialist studies. It is hoped that this type of exercise will make the student see the relationship between expression and content, and will therefore persuade him of the relevance of English learning to his own specialist field. In the last resort, the authors depend on the student being prepared to teach himself, to concentrate diligently on the features of language exemplified in the texts, and to approach the linguistic content of these books with the same spirit of enquiry and desire for knowledge as he would be expected to bring to the study of his speciality.

It is appreciated that, even in a course whose primary concern is with the written language, the teaching process must inevitably bring in the spoken form as well. Therefore, in order to assist both teacher and learner, the texts have been recorded on tape, as also have those exercises containing additional vocabulary, the pronunciation of which might otherwise pose a problem.

Edinburgh   J. P. B. A.
1974   H. G. W.

Introduction

1 Guide to the book

The book contains eight units, each of which is divided into five sections:

    I: Reading and comprehension
    II: Use of language
    III: Information transfer
    IV: Guided writing
    V: Free reading

Each of the five sections follows the same basic pattern.* This is as follows:

I READING AND COMPREHENSION

This section begins with a reading passage within which are inserted sets of comprehension checks in the form of statements which may or may not be correct. The learner has to decide on the correctness of each statement. These checks are inserted within the reading passage itself rather than at the end because we want to encourage the learner to think about what he reads *as* he reads and to pay close attention to what is actually expressed in the passage. Once the learner realizes that his understanding is going to be systematically checked in this way he is likely to read more attentively for meaning and to treat his reading not simply as a language exercise relevant only to the English class but as a technique for acquiring information which will be useful in a wider field of study.

    The comprehension checks require the learner to indicate whether a given statement is true or false according to the passage. But it is important that he should know *why* a statement is true or false and be able to recognize what it is in the passage that leads him to decide one way or the other. This is why each comprehension check is provided with a solution.

    The solutions refer the learner to those features of the reading passage which provide evidence for the truth or falsehood of the statements in the

---

* With the exception of Section I in Unit 8 where it was necessary to organize the material differently in order to give emphasis to the teaching points with which this section is concerned.

comprehension checks. They are explanations in that they point out what the reader must notice and how he must reason in order to arrive at the correct decision. Explanations of this kind are of course not necessary for someone who already has an efficient reading ability in English. At first glance it might appear that the solutions are sometimes too elaborate and detailed. But it must be remembered that the learner must be made aware of what is involved in reading with understanding before this ability can become habitual. What we aim to do by means of these solutions is to develop in the learner a reading strategy which he can apply generally to the texts he has to deal with as part of his study of engineering.

Sometimes a solution may serve simply to remind the learner of the know-ledge of English he already has. In Unit 3, for example, comprehension check (c) requires the learner to recognize that the same idea can be expressed by using different verbs, with appropriate changes in the postverbal structure. The solution appears as follows:

A force can start something moving.
= A force can cause something to move.
= A force can cause movement.

It is quite likely that the learner will be familiar with sentences of this type, and that he will have no difficulty in recognizing that 'A force can start something moving' means the same as 'A force can cause movement'. How-ever, the ability to recognize whether a given statement is true or not accord-ing to the passage does not come only from an understanding of the meaning of individual words and sentences. Very often it is a matter of recovering information which is implied rather than explicitly stated and of tracing the way in which what is expressed or implied in one sentence is related to what is expressed or implied in another. It is the function of many solutions, therefore, to make such implications explicit and to spell out the relationship between different statements.

Let us consider an example from Unit 4. Comprehension check (i) presents the following statement: 'If the mass of a body sliding over another is in-creased, the sliding friction force between them will also increase'. The student has to decide whether this statement is true or not with reference to the reading passage. In order to make this decision it is necessary to relate what is expressed in two different sentences: 15 and 18. This relating process is represented in the solution as follows (the symbols on the left indicate the kind of reasoning which is involved):

This shows that sliding friction is proportional to the reaction between the surfaces in contact. (18)

i.e. (*that is* If the reaction between the two surfaces in contact is increased,
to say) sliding friction is also increased.

but We can make the normal reaction between two surfaces in contact twice as large by doubling the mass carried by one surface. (15)

i.e.   The reaction between surfaces in contact increases as the mass carried by one surface increases.

∴   If the mass of a body sliding over another is increased, the (*therefore*) sliding friction force between them will also increase.

What solutions of this kind do, then, is to spell out certain reasoning processes which are employed by the efficient reader as a matter of habit. Moreover, they are the sort of processes which are overtly employed in many fields of scientific enquiry. Their use here as a language exercise is intended to appeal to the particular cognitive inclination of engineering students, and to make them see that the 'content' and the 'expression' of scientific writing are dependent upon each other.

The first three exercises following the reading passage are a logical development from the solutions. Each focuses on a feature of language use which is frequently referred to in the solutions and which is particularly relevant to an understanding of how English is used in written communication.

EXERCISE A *Rephrasing*

The object of this exercise is to make the student realize that writers commonly express the same idea in different ways and that there is no one-to-one correspondence between one linguistic form and one meaning. It is important that the student should realize this because two phrases may mean the same thing only within the context of a particular passage and it is therefore only by studying the context that the equivalence can be established. In Exercise A the student has to show how different forms function as synonymous expressions by replacing selected phrases in sentences with words from the reading passage which have the same meaning. For example (Unit 1, Exercise A) the following sentence is presented:

Chromium steels *resist* corrosion.

The student searches the reading passage and discovers the sentence 'Ceramics are often employed by engineers when materials which can withstand high temperatures are needed.' In this context *resist = withstand*, so the sentence in the exercise can be rephrased:

Chromium steels withstand corrosion.

In the same exercise we have the sentence

Chromium *can be included in* steel to provide a good cutting edge.

In this case two sentences in the reading passage are relevant: 'Certain elements can improve the properties of steel and are therefore added to it. For example, chromium may be included to resist corrosion. . . .' In this context *included in = added to* and *can = may*, so a suitable rephrasing of the sentence in the exercise is:

Chromium may be added to steel to provide a good cutting edge.

EXERCISE B *Contextual reference*

This exercise draws the learner's attention to the way pronouns and demonstratives are used to refer to something already mentioned and so serve to relate one statement to another in a text. Very often there is more than one grammatically possible connection between noun phrases and the reader has to decide which reference makes sense in the context of the passage concerned. The following example is from Unit 1:

> [2]Engineers must also understand the properties of these materials and how they can be worked.

The student's ability to assign the correct referential value to 'they' is tested as follows:
In sentence 2, 'they' refers to
  (a) the engineers
  (b) the materials.

Exercise B, then, obliges the learner to scrutinize the passage to assign the correct referential value to such anaphoric language items as pronouns, demonstratives and so on. This exercise is not difficult, and it may sometimes seem obvious what a given item refers to. But again it must be remembered that we are not just concerned with getting the learner to recognize the contextual reference of a particular language item in a particular passage but with developing a general ability to handle this feature of language use. The point is that this exercise directs the learner's attention to the way anaphoric devices work and so prepares him for those cases where identification of the referent is not so easy.

EXERCISE C *Relationships between statements* (Units 2–8)

Expressions like *therefore, consequently, however*, etc. indicate what function a particular sentence is meant to fulfil. A sentence which contains *therefore* is used to make a statement which follows logically from a previous statement. Similarly, *for example* indicates that the sentence is used to make a statement which illustrates a point made previously. Such expressions are explicit indicators of the communicative function of sentences. But writers do not use explicit indicators in every sentence. Very often a writer assumes that the reader will realize how a particular sentence is to be understood without the assistance of such indicators. It is of course crucial for the student learning to read a foreign language to understand which statements are meant to be illustrations, qualifications, conclusions and so on, and how statements are logically related to one another. The purpose of Exercise C is to make the learner aware of such communicative functions and of the way they are used in the development of written discourse.

In Exercise C the student proceeds in one of two ways. Sometimes he is provided with explicit indicators in the reading passage itself and he is required to replace these indicators with others which have an equivalent function. Thus in Unit 2, Exercise C he is given:

therefore (6)

In this case the student has simply to refer to sentence 6 in the reading passage, remove *then* and replace it with *therefore*:

Force, then, is a vector quantity

becomes

Force, therefore, is a vector quantity.

But it may not be a matter of simple replacement. Let us consider an example from Unit 3:

on the other hand (5)

It is possible to replace *also* in sentence 5 with the given phrase, but commas must be added and the resulting sentence sounds rather strained:

A force can, on the other hand, stop something moving or hinder motion.

A better solution is to put *on the other hand* at the beginning of the sentence and to delete *also*:

On the other hand a force can stop something moving or hinder motion.

In the above examples the student is required to replace one indicator with another of equivalent function. Elsewhere he is required to insert indicators so as to give statements an explicitness they would not otherwise have. In Unit 2 we have the following:

examples of (4)
thus (12)

Sentence 4 of the reading passage is:

Mass, volume and length are scalar quantities.

This can be shown explicitly as an exemplification by inserting the given indicator as follows:

Mass, volume and length are examples of scalar quantities.

Similarly, sentence 12 can be made explicit as a conclusion deriving from what has been stated previously:

Thus the line is vertical because the direction of the force it represents is vertical.

The central purpose of this exercise, then (notice *then!*), is to bring to the learner's notice the ways in which sentences are used to perform different acts of communication and how such acts are related to one another in the development of a discourse.

The exercises in section I are designed to make little demand on the learner's productive ability. Their purpose is to direct the learner to a discovery of what is involved in the comprehension of written communication. The exercises in sections II–IV are intended to extend comprehension into written work.

II USE OF LANGUAGE

The Use of Language section contains a variety of exercises of which two types call for special comment: statements based on diagrams and grammar practice.

Statements based on diagrams vary from unit to unit but all these exercises have the same basic aim. This aim is to guide the student to use his understanding of the reading passage to perform for himself the communicative acts which appear to be of particular importance in mechanical engineering. Thus in Unit 1 the learner is required to complete a diagram according to his understanding of the reading passage. When the diagram is completed it serves as a model for writing classifying sentences at various levels of generality. In Unit 2 diagrams are used for producing definitions, classifications and generalizations, and in the following units other acts of communication are presented in a similar way.

One type of activity which appears in section II might be called *rhetorical transformation*. This involves changing one mode of communication into another. For example, we see in Unit 2 that the definition:

A scalar quantity is a physical quantity which has magnitude but not direction

can be changed, or transformed, into a generalization:

A scalar quantity has magnitude but not direction.

Similarly, a pair of sentences of which one is an instruction and one a result can be transformed into an observation (Unit 3), or one or more observations can be transformed into a special kind of generalization called an induction (Unit 4).

As stated above in the editors' preface, it is assumed that the student already has a knowledge of basic grammar. It is also assumed that this knowledge will be consolidated during the course of the book as the student experiences language used in meaningful contexts. For these reasons no attempt has been made to provide a detailed review of English grammar. Instead, the grammar exercises in this section are designed to focus on points which are particularly important in the context of engineering, especially those points which may represent continuing 'trouble spots' for many students.

III INFORMATION TRANSFER

Information transfer is essentially a development of the exercises in section II. It brings the learner's attention to bear on problems which are related both to the subject matter and the language use of the preceding reading passage and exercises. To solve the problems the learner has to call upon his experience of both English and engineering and in providing a solution he is necessarily integrating the two areas of knowledge in a meaningful way. The aim of section III is to give the student practice in transferring information from one medium to another. For example, the student is asked to write recommendations based on a graph of a table (Unit 4), or design specifications based on a diagram (Unit 7). Elsewhere, he has to write inductions based on diagrams or tables (Unit 6) or, having been provided with appropriate vocabulary, he must describe the shapes of various engineering objects as completely as possible (Unit 8). This kind of exercise is of particular relevance to students of engineering, who are frequently required to convert information from tables, diagrams and graphs into verbal form, and the reverse.

IV GUIDED WRITING

The aim of the guided writing exercises is integrative rather than analytic; that is, the student uses a wide range of grammatical devices and sees how they combine to produce an integrated piece of writing. The guided writing sections vary in design, and become more difficult in the later units. A typical guided writing exercise is done in three stages. At the first stage the student examines various groups of words and combines each group into a sentence by following the clues provided. Some sentences are easy to write, some are more difficult; this reflects the situation in actual writing, where simple sentences alternate with more complex structures according to the nature of the message the writer wishes to convey. At the second stage the student creates a coherent text by rewriting the sentences in a logical order, deciding on paragraph divisions and adding various 'transitional' features where necessary. Thirdly, the student is presented with a number of diagrams which illustrate the passage. The student labels the diagrams and incorporates them into the passage, making any changes to the text that may be necessary. The guided writing is designed to allow some scope for the student to exercise his own judgement in the choice of words and structures, so there is no reason why the student's version should be identical to the one given in the key. If the paragraphs differ, the student should try to evaluate the relative merits of the two versions. Classroom discussion of these differences should help the student to develop a sense of style.

V FREE READING

This section consists of a passage of prose which is longer and more difficult than the reading passage in section I. The reason for including this section is to give the student an opportunity to learn for himself. The previous sections impose a fairly strict control over the student's activities; the free reading enables him to try out what he has learnt in his own way and his own time. No matter how carefully we develop our teaching procedures, it appears that learners develop their own individual way of learning, and the free reading passages are meant to give the reader a chance to think for himself without being imposed upon.* It is assumed that the reader's interest in the way language is used in an engineering context will have been sufficiently aroused in the preceding sections for him to be ready to apply his own intensive reading technique without specific directives in the form of further exercises. The free reading section provides additional opportunities for word study and gives the student a chance to try his skill in locating further examples of the points he has studied in the unit. It is hoped that the final section of each unit will provide a bridge to more extensive reading beyond the confines of this book, and that the student will be encouraged to consult his standard engineering texts as a further source of information about the way language is used.

2 Teaching suggestions

The following notes indicate how the second unit might be dealt with in the classroom; the other units can be handled in a similar way. These notes are intended to be suggestions only. It is expected that the teacher will develop his own procedures according to the needs of his students. A particular teacher, for example, may find that he needs to place greater emphasis on one type of exercise than on another. He may wish to pay more attention to oral than to written work, or the reverse. It will also be up to the teacher to decide, according to his own circumstances, how the work is to be divided into class sessions, and which part of it can most appropriately be done as homework.

I READING AND COMPREHENSION

(i) Reading the text
Get the class to read sentences 1–7 by themselves.
Do questions (a) and (b) with them so that it is clear what they have to do.
Get the class to do questions (c) and (d) on their own.
Choose one student. Ask him whether he has written down 'true' or 'not true' for question (c). Get him to justify his decision with reference to the appropriate parts of the text. Ask other students whether they agree, and if not why not. Get the class to turn to the relevant solution. Read it aloud to the class while the students follow it in their books.
Choose another student, and do the same with question (d).
Read sentences 1–7 aloud to the class, while they follow in their books.
Get the class to read sentences 8–14 by themselves.
Get the class to do questions (e)–(h) on their own, and repeat the process as for questions (c) and (d).

* For those teachers who prefer to supplement free reading with more formal practice, a set of comprehension questions for all the free reading passages is provided on p. 103.

Read the whole passage aloud to the class, without the questions, while the students follow in their books.

(ii) Exercises
EXERCISE A *Rephrasing*

Get the class to do the exercise in their notebooks.
When the class have finished the exercise, write the first sentence on the board. Underline the expression which is to be replaced.
Select a volunteer to come to the board and write in the replacing expression above the words which are underlined.
Ask the class to judge whether the rephrasing is appropriate. Consider alternatives if necessary.
Bracket together the appropriate replacement(s) with the original expression as follows:

We $\begin{Bmatrix} \text{calculate} \\ \text{measure} \end{Bmatrix}$ mass in kilogrammes.

Do the remaining sentences in the same way.

EXERCISE B *Contextual reference*

Get the class to do the exercise in their notebooks.
Ask the class to show which choices they have made in question 1 by putting up their hands.
Ask students to replace the item indicated with the phrase they have chosen, and read out the sentence which results. For example, a student choosing 2(a) will read out 'Scalar and vector quantities have size, or magnitude, but only vector quantities possess direction.' A student choosing 2(b) will read out 'Physical quantities have size, or magnitude, but only vector quantities possess direction.'
Ask the class to judge which statement is correct.
Repeat the process for the other questions.

EXERCISE C *Relationships between statements*

Get the class to do the exercise in their notebooks.
When the class have finished the exercise, write sentence 4 on the board.
Select a volunteer to come to the board and indicate the change.
Ask the class to judge whether the change is correct.
Do the remaining sentences.
The following methods of indicating a change may be used:

examples of
Mass, volume and length are ∧ scalar quantities.
  therefore
Force, ~~then~~ , is a vector quantity.

Although
∧   Both have size or magnitude, ~~but~~ only vector quantities possess
direction.

II USE OF LANGUAGE
EXERCISE A *Classification of physical quantities*

Get the class to copy out and complete the diagram, and use it to write out
sentences in their notebooks as instructed.
Put the diagram on the board and complete it with the students' help. Get
the students to correct their own diagrams.
Get the individual students to read out the sentences they have written.

EXERCISE B *Making definitions*

Get the students to study the diagram and read the explanation carefully.
Do the sentences orally.
Get the students to write the sentences in their notebooks. While they are
doing this, go round the class and give individual help where necessary.

EXERCISES C and D

Proceed as in Exercise B.

III INFORMATION TRANSFER
EXERCISE A *Changing vector diagrams to written descriptions*

Allow the students several minutes to study the example.
Do one or two sentences orally.
Tell the students to write the sentences in their notebooks. They should write
all the sentences, including the ones given in the text.

EXERCISE B *Sentence building*

Get the students to read the example and write the sentences in their notebooks.
Select students to read out their versions. Use the students' answers to write
a correct version of each sentence on the board.

IV GUIDED WRITING
STAGE 1 *The use of the passive in the description of an experiment*

Get the students to read the explanation carefully.
Do one or two sentences orally.
Tell the students to write all the sentences in their notebooks. Give individual
help where necessary.
Taking the sentences one by one, get individual students to read out what
they have written. Write the correct version of each sentence on the board.

STAGE 2 *Paragraph building*

Get the students to write a paragraph in their notebooks, following the instructions. Tell them to label the diagram and include it in the paragraph. After the students have written their paragraphs, get the class to number the sentences on the board in the correct order.

Invite one of the students to copy the diagram onto the board and to label it. Get the class to suggest a suitable title for the paragraph.

Discuss any differences between the students' versions and the version in the key.

Give the students time to change their own paragraphs where necessary.

V FREE READING

Tell the students to read the passage in their own time.

Encourage them to look for points of interest in the text and to relate them to the exercises in this and other units.

Tell the students to make a note of any unfamiliar words and to look them up in their dictionaries. Get them to practise using these words in sentences of their own.

Repeat this process with further passages selected from standard texts used by the students in their engineering classes.

RECORDING

Recordings of the reading passages and the answers to those grammar exercises in Section II which contain the most difficult vocabulary are available on cassette from Oxford University Press.

A useful revision exercise is to play the recordings of the reading passages while the students follow the text in their books. If it is necessary to develop the learners' ability to comprehend spoken English, follow this up by giving comprehension questions orally. (See pages 103–4 for questions relating to the free reading sections.) Recordings of answers to the grammar questions will serve as a model if the teacher wishes to do these exercises orally.

1 Engineering Materials

I READING AND COMPREHENSION

[1]Engineers have to know the best and most economical materials to use. [2]Engineers must also understand the properties of these materials and how they can be worked. [3]There are two kinds of materials used in engineering – metals and non-metals. [4]We can divide metals into ferrous and non-ferrous metals. [5]The former contain iron and the latter do not contain iron. [6]Cast iron and steel, which are both alloys, or mixtures of iron and carbon, are the two most important ferrous metals. [7]Steel contains a smaller proportion of carbon than cast iron contains. [8]Certain elements can improve the properties of steel and are therefore added to it. [9]For example, chromium may be included to resist corrosion and tungsten to increase hardness. [10]Aluminium, copper, and the alloys, bronze and brass, are common non-ferrous metals.

Study the following statements carefully and write down whether they are true or not true according to the information expressed above. Then check your answers by referring to solutions at the end of the passage.*

(a) Non-metals are used by engineers.
(b) Cast iron contains more carbon than steel.
(c) Chromium improves the properties of steel.
(d) Copper contains iron.
(e) Bronze is an alloy.

[11]Plastics and ceramics are non-metals; however, plastics may be machined like metals. [12]Plastics are classified into two types – thermoplastics and thermosets. [13]Thermoplastics can be shaped and reshaped by heat and

---

* The following symbols are used in the solutions:
    $=$ equals, means the same as
    $\neq$ does not equal, mean the same as
    i.e. that is to say
    $\therefore$ therefore

pressure but thermosets cannot be reshaped because they undergo chemical changes as they harden. [14]Ceramics are often employed by engineers when materials which can withstand high temperatures are needed.

(f)   Thermosets can be machined.
(g)   Thermoplastics are metals.
(h)   Ceramics can withstand high temperatures.

Solutions

(a)   There are two kinds of materials used in engineering – metals and non-metals. (3)
=   metals and non-metals are used in engineering
∴   metals and non-metals are used by engineers
∴   *Non-metals are used by engineers.*

(b)   Steel contains a smaller proportion of carbon than cast iron contains. (7)
∴   Cast iron contains a larger proportion of carbon than steel.
=   *Cast iron contains more carbon than steel.*

(c)   Certain elements can improve the properties of steel and are therefore added to it. (8) For example, chromium may be included. . . . (9)
i.e.   Chromium is an example of the elements which are added to steel and can improve the properties of steel.
∴   *Chromium improves the properties of steel.*

(d)   Aluminium, copper and the alloys, bronze and brass, are common non-ferrous metals. (10)
i.e.   Copper is a non-ferrous metal.
but   non-ferrous = does not contain iron
∴   It is NOT TRUE that copper contains iron.

(e)   Aluminium, copper and the alloys, bronze and brass, are common non-ferrous metals. (10)
i.e.   Bronze and brass are alloys.
∴   *Bronze is an alloy.*

(f)   Plastics and ceramics are non-metals; however, plastics may be machined like metals. (11)
may be = can be
∴   Plastics can be machined.
Plastics are classified into two types – thermoplastics and thermosets. (12)
i.e.   Thermosets are a kind of plastic.
∴   *Thermosets can be machined.*

(g) Plastics can be classified into two types – thermoplastics and thermosets. (12)

i.e. Thermoplastics are a kind of plastic.

∴   It is NOT TRUE that thermoplastics are metals.

(h) Ceramics are often employed by engineers when materials which can
withstand high temperatures are needed. (14)

i.e. Engineers use ceramics when they need materials which can withstand
high temperatures.

∴   *Ceramics can withstand high temperatures.*

EXERCISE A *Rephrasing*

Rewrite the following sentences, replacing the words printed in italics with
expressions from the passage which have a similar meaning.

EXAMPLE

There are two kinds of *engineering materials*.
There are two kinds of *materials used in engineering*.

1. Nickel steel is *a mixture* of iron, carbon and nickel.
2. Chromium *can be included in* steel to provide a good cutting edge.
3. There are many *kinds* of steel used in industry.
4. Ceramics are *used* by engineers where heat-resistant materials are needed.
5. Chromium steels *resist* corrosion.

EXERCISE B *Contextual reference*

1. In sentence 2, 'they' refers to
   (a) the engineers
   (b) the materials

2. In sentence 5, 'the former' refers to
   (a) ferrous metals
   (b) non-ferrous metals

3. In sentence 5, 'the latter' refers to
   (a) ferrous metals
   (b) non-ferrous metals

4. In sentence 8, 'it' refers to
   (a) steel
   (b) iron

5. In sentence 13, 'they' refers to
   (a) plastics
   (b) thermosets
   (c) thermoplastics

II   USE OF LANGUAGE

EXERCISE A *Classification of engineering materials*

Draw in your notebook the diagram below and complete it, using the information from the reading passage.

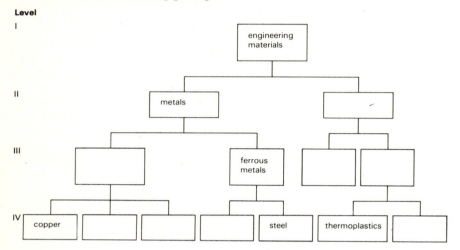

Note that this diagram *classifies* engineering materials at four levels of generality. Look at the following sentences:
  1. Steel is a ferrous metal.
  2. Iron and steel are ferrous metals.
  3. Steel is an engineering material.
  4. Steel is a metal.
  5. Ferrous metals are engineering materials.
  6. Metals are engineering materials.

Now write as many sentences as you can like those above based on the completed diagram.

EXERCISE B *Classification (continued)*

Draw diagrams to classify the items in the following lists. Each diagram should have three levels.

  1. alloys, copper, brass, pure metals, aluminium, metals.
  2. brazing, electric-arc welding, soldering, metal-joining methods, welding, oxy-acetylene welding.
  3. measuring instruments, non-precision instruments, micrometer, vernier gauge, metre stick, precision instruments, slip blocks, foot-rule.

4. units of area, cubic metre, metric units, millimetre, square metre, linear units, kilometre, units of volume.
5. milling machines, copy-miller, shaping machines, drilling machines, vertical shaper, radial arm drill, machine tools.
6. petrol engines, external-combustion engines, diesel engines, heat engines, steam turbines, internal-combustion engines.
7. grinding, metal cleaning methods, acid cleaning, mechanical methods, grit-blasting, alkali cleaning, chemical methods.
8. regular shapes, square, triangle, oval, irregular shapes, shapes.
9. adhesive joints, inseparable joints, welded joints, nut and bolt joints, joints, riveted joints, separable joints.
10. forging, sand casting, die casting, production processes, rolling, casting.

Now use the diagrams you have made to write paragraphs like the following:

EXAMPLE
    Metals can be classified as pure metals and alloys. Copper and aluminium are examples of pure metals and brass is an example of an alloy.

EXERCISE C *However, therefore, because*

In this book you will meet many words which can be used to connect statements. Three of the most common are:

(1) however   (2) therefore   (3) because

Look at these examples:
(1) (a) Copper does not rust.
     (b) Copper corrodes.
  (a+b) Copper does not rust; however it corrodes.
(2) (a) Cast iron is a brittle metal.
     (b) Cast iron is not used to withstand impact loads.
  (a+b) Cast iron is a brittle metal, therefore it is not used to withstand impact loads.
(3) (a) Titanium is used for aircraft frames.
     (b) Titanium is light and strong.
  (a+b) Titanium is used for aircraft frames because it is light and strong.

In (1), statement (b) qualifies statement (a)
In (2), statement (b) is a result of statement (a)
In (3), statement (b) gives the reason why statement (a) is true.

Now join each of the following pairs of statements. Write down your answers in your notebook, using 'however', 'therefore' or 'because' as in the examples.

1. Chromium resists corrosion.
   Chromium is added to steels to make them rust proof.
2. Cutting tools are made from high-speed steels.
   High-speed steels retain their cutting edge at high temperatures.
   (. . . these steels . . . .)
3. Under normal conditions aluminium resists corrosion.
   Serious corrosion occurs in salt water.
   (. . . serious corrosion . . . .)
4. Manganese steel is very hard.
   Manganese steel is used for armour plate.
5. Bronze has a low coefficient of friction.
   Bronze is used to make bearings.
6. Nylon is used to make fibres and gears.
   Nylon is tough and has a low coefficient of friction.
7. Tin is used to coat other metals to protect them.
   Tin resists corrosion.
8. Tin is expensive.
   The coats of tin applied to other metals are very thin.
   (. . . the coats of tin . . . .)
9. Stainless steels require little maintenance and have a high strength.
   Stainless steels are expensive and difficult to machine at high speeds.
10. Nickel, cobalt and chromium improve the properties of metals.
    Nickel, cobalt and chromium are added to steels.

EXERCISE D *Language of measurement* (i): *Basic metric units*

Study the diagrams and memorize the examples.

linear dimensions A linear dimension is one which we can measure in a straight line.

3m

(a) length

We can describe the length of this bar in four ways:
   The bar is three metres long.
   The bar is three metres in length.
   The bar has a length of three metres.
   The length of the bar is three metres.

(b) width or breadth

We can describe the width or breadth of this driving belt in four ways:

   The belt is sixty millimetres wide/broad.
   The belt is sixty millimetres in width/breadth.
   The belt has a width/breadth of sixty millimetres.
   The width/breadth of the belt is sixty millimetres.

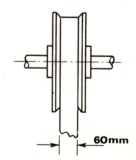

60mm

(c) height

We can describe the height of this
support tower in four ways:
    The tower is a hundred metres high.
    The tower is a hundred metres in height.
    The tower has a height of a hundred
metres.
    The height of the tower is a hundred
metres.

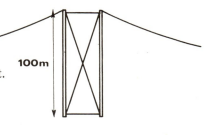

(d) thickness

We can describe the thickness of this steel
sheet in three ways:
    The sheet is three millimetres thick.
    The sheet has a thickness of three
millimetres.
    The thickness of the sheet is three
millimetres.

(e) depth   Depth is usually measured vertically downwards from a surface.
This surface is often ground level or the surface of a liquid.

We can describe the depth of this trench in
four ways:
    The trench is two metres deep.
    The trench is two metres in depth.
    The trench has a depth of two metres.
    The depth of the trench is two metres.

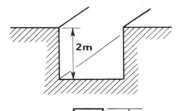

Other examples of depth:

(i) The depth of the beam is three hundred
millimetres.

(ii) The depth of the screw thread is one
point seven five millimetres.

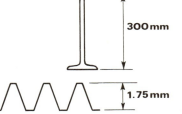

mass

We can describe the mass of this block in three ways:
    The block has a mass of fifty kilogrammes.
    The block is of mass fifty kilogrammes.
    The mass of the block is fifty kilogrammes.

EXERCISE E *Language of measurement* (ii): *Derived metric units*

Study the diagrams and memorize the examples.

Derived metric units are products of the basic units.

area Area is measured in squared linear units,
for example, square metres – m².

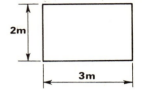

We can describe the area of this steel plate in
three ways:
    The plate has an area of six square metres.
    The plate is six square metres in area.
    The area of the plate is six square metres.

volume Volume is measured in cubed linear units, for example cubic
metres – m³. The volume of a liquid may be measured in litres and sub-
divisions of a litre.

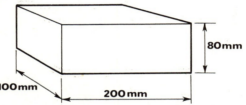

We can describe the volume of this brick in three ways:
    The brick has a volume of 1600 cubic centimetres.
    The brick is 1600 cubic centimetres in volume.
    The volume of the brick is 1600 cubic centimetres.

capacity Capacity is the ability of a container to hold something. Like
volume it is measured in cubed linear units. For liquids, litres and sub-
divisions of a litre may be used.

We can describe the capacity of this tank in three ways:
    The tank has a capacity of twenty-four cubic metres.
    The tank is twenty-four cubic metres in capacity.
    The capacity of the tank is twenty-four cubic metres.

EXERCISE F *Language of measurement* (iii): *Compound metric units*

Look again at the diagrams on pages 6–8 and the language used to describe the diagrams. Copy the following table into your notebook and complete it by filling in the spaces.

physical quantity	typical unit	short form
force	newton	N
time		s
	kilogramme	
length and distance		
	square metre	
		m³

Compound units are made up of basic and derived units of measurement.
(a) The stroke / means 'per', and indicates that the unit in front of the stroke is divided by the unit after the stroke.
(b) Where there is no stroke between two units, the units are multiplied together.

Now rewrite the following sentences completing them by filling in the spaces.

EXAMPLE
  moments   The moment of a force is measured in newton metres.
    Short form = Nm
    The moment of a force is found by multiplying a force by a distance.

1. *velocity*   Velocity is measured in metres per second.
      Short form = ...
      Velocity is found by ... a ... by a ...
2. *pressure*   Pressure is measured in ... per ...
      Short form = N/m^2
      Pressure is found by ... a ... by a ...
3. *density*   Density is measured in kilogrammes ... cubic metre.
      Short form = ...
      Density is found by dividing a ... by ...
4. *stress*   Stress is measured in newtons per ...
      Short form = N/mm^2
      Stress is found by ... a ... by an area
5. *acceleration*   Acceleration is measured in metres per second squared.
      Short form = ...
      Acceleration is found by ... a ... by a time.

III INFORMATION TRANSFER

EXERCISE A *Describing dimensions*

Describe the following objects in as many ways as you can.

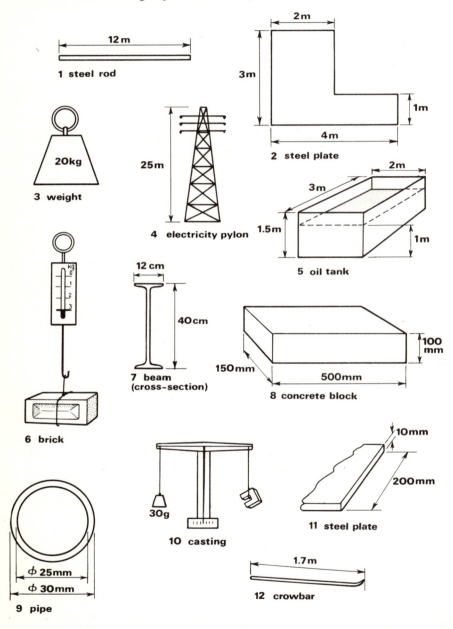

1 steel rod

2 steel plate

3 weight

4 electricity pylon

5 oil tank

6 brick

7 beam (cross-section)

8 concrete block

9 pipe

10 casting

11 steel plate

12 crowbar

IV GUIDED WRITING

STAGE 1 *Sentence building*

Join the following groups of sentences to make eleven longer sentences, using the connecting words printed at the beginning of each group (except group 6). You may omit words and make whatever changes you think are necessary in the word order and punctuation of the sentences.

EXAMPLE
BECAUSE/AND/HOWEVER
Plastics are used widely in engineering.
They are cheap.
They have a resistance to atmospheric corrosion.
Plastics are not particularly strong.
= Plastics are used widely in engineering because they are cheap and have a resistance to atmospheric corrosion; however they are not particularly strong.

1. AND
   There are two types of plastics.
   Thermoplastics are plastics.
   Thermosets are plastics.

2. AND/WHEREAS/AND
   Thermoplastics will soften when heated.
   Thermoplastics will harden when cooled.
   Thermosets set on heating.
   Thermosets will not remelt.

3. FROM/TO
   Plastics are used to make a great variety of products.
   Plastics are used to make textiles.
   Plastics are used to make engineering components.

4. SUCH AS
   Plastics are available in many forms.
   Plastics are available in the form of sheets, tubes, rods, moulding powders and resins.

5. TO
   Various methods are used.
   These methods convert raw plastic into finished products.

6. Compression moulding is a common method.
   Compression moulding is used for shaping thermosets.

7. WITH/WHICH
   The equipment consists of a press.

The press has two heated platens.
The two heated platens carry an upper and a lower mould.

8. THEN
Powder is placed in the lower mould.
This is moulding powder.
The upper mould is pressed down on the lower mould.

9. TO/WHICH
The pressure and the heat change the powder.
The powder becomes liquid plastic.
The liquid plastic fills the space between the moulds.

10. WHEN/AND
The chemical changes have taken place.
The mould is opened.
The moulding is extracted.

11. BY
Plastic bowls are made.
The compression moulding method is used,

STAGE 2 *Paragraph building*

Now group the completed sentences into two paragraphs and give a title to
the passage. Include the example as the first sentence of your passage.

V   FREE READING

Read the following passage in your own time. If there are any words you
do not know, look them up in your dictionary. Try to find additional examples
of the points you have studied in this unit.

CORROSION

Corrosion attacks all engineering materials, especially metals. Corrosion is
any chemical action which harms the properties of a material. It reduces the
life of a material and increases the cost of a structure. For example, a steel
bridge must be repainted regularly to protect it from rust. Various metals
have therefore been developed to resist corrosion. Among them are the
stainless steels. These metals contain from 12 to 35% chromium which
forms a very thin layer or film of chromium oxide on the surface of the
metal. This film protects the metal from corrosion. Alloys made from
copper and nickel are also corrosion-resistant. For example Monel metal,
which contains roughly 60% nickel and 30% copper, is resistant to both
fresh and salt water corrosion. It is therefore used for marine engine parts,

and for other surfaces like ships' propellers which are in contact with sea water. Cupronickels, which contain a smaller proportion of nickel, have a similar resistance to fresh and sea water. They are mainly used to make tubes.

When two different metals touch each other in the presence of moisture, corrosion occurs. This type of corrosion is known as galvanic or electrolytic corrosion because it has an electrical cause. The metals and the moisture act like a weak battery and the chemical action which results corrodes one of the metals. If, for example, aluminium sheets are riveted with copper rivets, the aluminium near the rivets will corrode in damp conditions.

No material can be completely corrosion-resistant. Even stainless steels will corrode. Engineers can, however, fight corrosion. For example, they can use high-purity metals because these metals are more resistant than alloys. They can also make sure that two dissimilar metals are not allowed to touch each other. Finally engineers can protect the surfaces of the metals in many different ways. One of the most common methods is to paint them.

2 Vectors

[1]We deal with many different physical quantities in engineering. [2]They can be divided into two groups – scalar and vector quantities. [3]Both have size, or magnitude, but only vector quantities possess direction. [4]Mass, volume and length are scalar quantities. [5]Force, which we measure in newtons, possesses magnitude and direction. [6]Force, then, is a vector quantity. [7]Other examples are acceleration and velocity.

(a) There are two physical quantities in engineering.
(b) Scalar quantities have magnitude.
(c) Acceleration has direction.
(d) There are only three vector quantities in engineering.

[8]Any vector quantity can be represented by a vector. [9]The straight line a–b in the diagram is a vector which represents a force. [10]If we calculate its length we find that it is proportional to the magnitude of the force. [11]The direction of the line indicates the direction of the force. [12]The line is vertical because the direction of the force it represents is vertical. [13]It is important also to know in what sense of direction the force is acting. [14]The arrow-head on the line shows that the sense of direction of the force is upwards.

(e) We can use a vector to represent velocity.
(f) The straight line a–b in the diagram is a force.

(g) The arrow-head on line *a–b* shows that the force is acting in a vertical direction.

(h) The longer the line *a–b*, the greater the force it represents.

Solutions

(a) We deal with many different physical quantities in engineering (1).

i.e. There are many physical quantities in engineering. '

∴ There are MORE THAN TWO physical quantities in engineering.

(b) Both have size, or magnitude, but only vector quantities possess direction. (3)

i.e. Scalar quantities have size, or magnitude.

and Vector quantities have size, or magnitude.

size = magnitude

∴ *Scalar quantities have magnitude.*

(c) Other examples are acceleration and velocity. (7)

i.e. Other examples of vector quantities are acceleration and velocity.

∴ Acceleration is a vector quantity.

but Vector quantities have direction.

∴ *Acceleration has direction.*

(d) Force, then, is a vector quantity. (6) Other examples are acceleration and velocity. (7)

i.e. Force, acceleration and velocity are examples of vector quantities.

≠ Force, acceleration and velocity are the only vector quantities.

∴ It is NOT TRUE that there are only three vector quantities in engineering.

(e) Any vector quantity can be represented by a vector. (8)

but Velocity is a vector quantity. (See **(c)**.)

∴ *We can use a vector to represent velocity.*

(f) The straight line *a–b*, in the diagram, is a vector which represents a force. (9)

i.e. The straight line *a–b*, in the diagram, is a vector.

∴ The straight line *a–b*, in the diagram, is NOT a force.

(g) The line is vertical because the direction of the force it represents is vertical. (12)

i.e. The direction of the line shows that the force is acting in a vertical direction.

The arrow-head on the line shows that the sense of direction of the force is upwards. (14)

i.e. The arrow-head shows that the force is acting upwards and not downwards.

∴ The arrow-head on line *a–b* does NOT show that the force is acting in a vertical direction.

(h)   If we calculate its length we find that it is proportional to the magnitude of the force. (10)

=   The length of the line is proportional to the magnitude of the force it represents.

∴   *The longer the line a–b, the greater the force it represents.*

EXERCISE A *Rephrasing*

Rewrite the following, replacing the words printed in italics with expressions from the passage which have a similar meaning.

1. We *calculate* mass in kilogrammes.
2. The arrow-head *indicates* the sense of direction of the force.
3. Scalar quantities *have* magnitude but not direction.
4. The direction of the line *shows* the direction of the force.
5. The *size* of the force is 10 N.

EXERCISE B *Contextual reference*

1. In sentence 2, 'they' refers to   (a) physical quantities
   (b) two groups

2. In sentence 3, 'both' refers to   (a) scalar and vector quantities
   (b) physical quantities

3. In sentence 10, 'it' refers to   (a) the length
   (b) the force

4. In sentence 10, 'its' refers to   (a) the force's
   (b) the line's

5. In sentence 12, 'it' refers to   (a) the force
   (b) the line

EXERCISE C *Relationships between statements*

Place the following expressions in the sentences indicated. Replace and re-order the words in the sentences where necessary.

EXAMPLE   although (3)

   Both have size, or magnitude, *but* only vector quantities possess direction.

=   *Although* both have size, or magnitude, only vector quantities possess direction.

examples of (4)   in addition (11)
therefore (6)   thus (12)
for example (9)   for this reason (14)

II USE OF LANGUAGE

EXERCISE A *Classification of physical quantities*

Copy the following diagram into your notebook and complete it to make a classification of physical quantities. Use the information from the reading passage to help you.

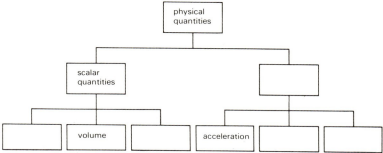

Use the completed diagram to make classifying sentences.

EXAMPLE
   Volume is a scalar quantity.

EXERCISE B *Making definitions*

Study the following diagram:

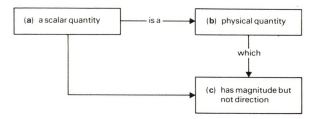

We can make a classifying sentence about a scalar quantity by joining **(a)** and **(b)**:

   A scalar quantity is a physical quantity.

We can then expand the sentence by including **(c)**:

   A scalar quantity is a physical quantity which has magnitude but not direction.

The expanded sentence defines a scalar quantity. It is a *definition*. Now write as many definitions as you can using the following table.

a	b	c
a vector quantity		can extend a body
a load		has magnitude and direction
a tensile force	straight line	represents a vector quantity
a linear dimension	force	is a product of basic units
a vector	unit	can be measured in a straight line
a compressive force	dimension	can stretch or compress a body
a derived unit	physical quantity	can compress a body
friction		opposes motion

EXERCISE C *Making generalizations*

When we join (a) and (c) only we make a type of statement called a *generalization*.

EXAMPLE

A scalar quantity has magnitude but not direction.

Now write as many generalizations as you can based on the table.

EXERCISE D *Lower-level and higher-level generalizations*

Statements which contain higher-level items are more *general* than statements which contain lower-level items. Look at the following example:

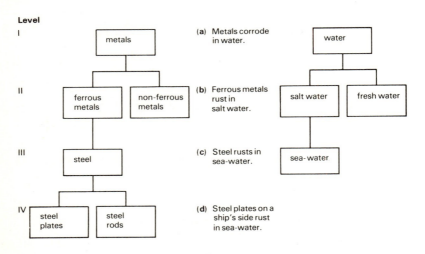

Statement (a) is the most general statement. When statement (a) is true, statements (b), (c) and (d) must also be true.

Study the following sentences. Column (a) contains statements with lower-level items. Column (b) contains more general statements with higher-level items. Write column (a) in your notebook then match each lower-level statement with a general statement from column (b).

EXAMPLE

Iron rusts.   Metals corrode.

a	b
1. Iron rusts.	Engines consume fuel.
2. Bronze contains copper and tin.	Metallic elements are added to steel to improve its properties.
3. A square metre is made by multiplying a metre by a metre.	Compressive forces shorten bodies.
4. Chromium makes steel corrosion-resistant.	Metals corrode.
5. A load of five tonnes compresses a concrete column.	Derived units are products of basic units.
6. Zirconia heat shields withstand temperatures over 2000°C.	Alloys are mixtures of metals.
7. Vinylite can be shaped in a lathe.	Ceramics can resist high temperatures.
8. Railway lines extend in hot weather.	Plastics may be machined.
9. Four-stroke internal-combustion engines burn petrol, diesel oil, and gas.	Metals expand when heated.

III INFORMATION TRANSFER

EXERCISE A *Changing vector diagrams to written descriptions*

Express the following vector diagrams in words. Write your answers down in your notebooks as in the example.

EXAMPLE

a–b is a vector.
It represents a force of five newtons.
The force acts in an upwards direction
at thirty degrees to the horizontal.

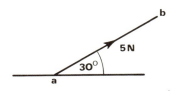

1.

The force acts vertically upwards.

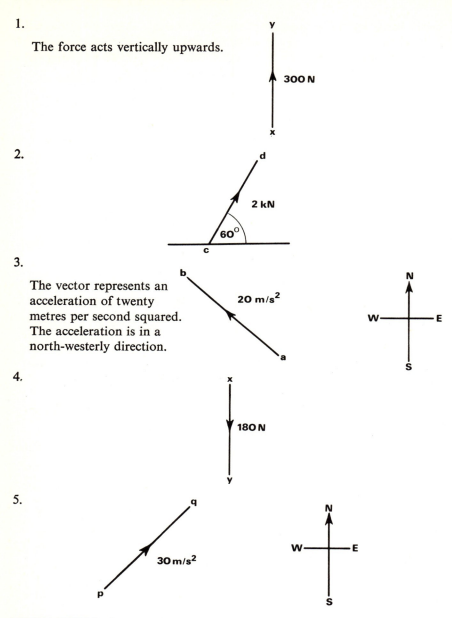

2.

3.

The vector represents an
acceleration of twenty
metres per second squared.
The acceleration is in a
north-westerly direction.

4.

5.

EXERCISE B *Sentence building*

Now join each set of three statements into a single sentence.

EXAMPLE

a–b is a vector.

It represents a force of five newtons.

The force acts in an upwards direction at thirty degrees to the horizontal.

= *a–b* is a vector which represents a force of five newtons acting in an upwards direction at thirty degrees to the horizontal.

IV GUIDED WRITING

STAGE 1 *The use of the passive in the description of an experiment*

Look at this sentence:

(a) Bill and I measured the extension in the steel bar.

We would not normally write this type of sentence in a report on an engineering experiment. Instead we would write:

(b) The extension in the steel bar was measured.

Sentence (b) is an example of the passive construction. The passive is common in scientific writing where the action described is felt to be more important than the actors.

Look at the following examples of active and passive sentences:

active	*passive*
We suspend a 1 kg mass from a light bar.	A 1 kg mass is suspended from a light bar.
We measured the distance between the mass and the fulcrum.	The distance between the mass and the fulcrum was measured.
We may calculate the moment of the force in two ways.	The moment of the force may be calculated in two ways.

Now rewrite each of the following sentences in the passive.
1. If we place a smooth roller on an inclined plane, it will run down the plane.
2. Two other forces act on the roller.
3. We can apply this force in any direction providing one component acts up the plane.
4. We call the third force the normal reaction – R.
5. We can therefore draw a triangle of forces for the system.
6. The diagram shows this force – P – acting parallel to the plane.
   (In the diagram, this force . . . .)
7. To keep the roller in equilibrium we must apply a force to it.
   (A force . . . .)

8. One is the force due to gravity – F_g – which we can consider to act vertically downwards through the midpoint of the roller.
9. We now find that we have an example of a three-force system.
   (It . . . now . . . that we . . . .)
10. As we assume the roller and plane to be absolutely smooth, this reaction is at right angles to the surface of the plane.

STAGE 2 *Paragraph building*

Draw the following diagram and label the forces P, R, and F_g on it. Then rearrange the passive sentences so that they make a logical paragraph of which your diagram is the illustration. Sentence 1 is already in the correct position.

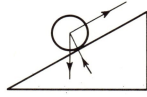

V   FREE READING

Read the following passage in your own time. If there are any words you do not know, look them up in your dictionary. Try to find additional examples of the points you have studied in this and other units.

SCALES AND GRAPHS

In engineering it is often necessary to describe quantities and relationships. We can give a pictorial representation of vector quantities by using vectors as described in the first reading passage in this unit. Scalar quantities are simply described by giving their magnitude in a suitable unit of measurement. For example, we can describe the mass of a body as a quantity of grammes, the capacity of a container as a number of cubic metres and a period of time as so many seconds. We can also illustrate scalar quantities by points or divisions on a scale. Thus, a clock is a scale for measuring time and the clock hands indicate the passage of time. Similarly a metre stick is a scale for measuring length and a thermometer is a scale for measuring heat.

Scales can also be used to make calculations. For example, engineers use slide-rules for quick multiplication and division. The slide-rule consists of two logarithmic scales.

When there is a relationship between two sets of observations, we can often express this as a mathematical formula. We can also use a graph.

A graph gives a visual representation of the relationship. This is often more easily understood than a law. For example, if we make a graph to compare the safe working loads of steel ropes with the circumference of the ropes, it is easy to see how the safe working load varies with the circumference. In addition we can use the graph as an information store, rather like a simple computer. In this way a graph can present at a glance the information contained in a law or a collection of tables.

A more complex kind of graph is the nomograph. This can show the relationship between more than two variables. A simple nomograph can consist of a number of scales arranged in a special shape. For example, three scales could be placed parallel to each other or in the form of the letter N, or even in curves. Such a nomograph is read by drawing a straight line to cut through all three scales. With a nomograph of this type an engineer could correlate information on the horse-power of a motor, its speed, and the diameter of driving shaft necessary to transmit the motor's power.

More complex nomographs are made on special graph paper and may even be in three dimensions.

3 Force

[1]We can describe a force only by its effects. [2]It cannot be measured directly like a length. [3]A force can start something moving. [4]If we push against a small object it moves. [5]A force can also stop something moving or hinder motion. [6]If we brake a moving car it slows down and will eventually stop. [7]Suspend a heavy mass from a copper wire. [8]The wire extends, showing that a force can stretch a body. [9]Forces may also compress, bend or even break an object.

(a) Length can be measured directly.
(b) A force can slow down a moving object.
(c) A force can cause movement.
(d) A body can be compressed by a force.
(e) A heavy mass can exert a force.

[10]A force can be one of attraction. [11]The force of attraction exerted by the huge mass of the earth is called gravity. [12]If we pick up a stone, then release it, it falls to the ground because of gravitational force. [13]Gravity is an example of a natural force. [14]Whether a force is naturally or deliberately exerted it cannot exist by itself. [15]Forces must always occur in pairs, never in isolation. [16]When a force acts on a rigid body it is balanced by an equal reaction force which acts in the opposite direction. [17]If a man stands on a slippery surface and brings a force to bear on a heavy load, the reaction force makes him slide backwards. [18]Similarly if a man fires a rifle, the force which pushes the bullet forwards will be matched by a force which makes the gun push backwards against his shoulder.

(f) Gravity is a force.
(g) Deliberately exerted forces can exist alone.
(h) Natural forces are forces of attraction.
(i) When a force acts on a rigid body, the magnitude of the reaction force depends on the size of the rigid body.

(j) The force which pushes a gun backwards when it is fired is a reaction force.

Solutions

(a) It cannot be measured directly like a length. (2)
i.e. A force cannot be measured directly but a length can be measured directly.
∴ *Length can be measured directly.*

(b) A force can also stop something moving or hinder motion. (5)
= A force can stop something moving.
and A force can slow down something which is moving.
∴ *A force can slow down a moving object.*

(c) A force can start something moving. (3)
= A force can cause something to move.
= *A force can cause movement.*

(d) Forces may also compress, bend or even break an object. (9)
i.e. An object can be compressed, bent or broken by a force.
an object (here) = a body
∴ *A body can be compressed by a force.*

(e) Suspend a heavy mass from a copper wire. (7) The wire extends . . . . (8)
i.e. The wire extends because the heavy mass is suspended from it.
. . . showing that a force can stretch a body. (8)
i.e. It is the force exerted by the heavy mass that stretches the wire.
∴ *A heavy mass can exert a force.*

(f) The force of attraction exerted by the huge mass of the earth is called gravity. (11)
i.e. Gravity is a force.

(g) Whether a force is naturally or deliberately exerted it cannot exist by itself. (14)
i.e. A naturally exerted force cannot exist by itself.
and A deliberately exerted force cannot exist by itself.
by itself = alone
∴ Deliberately exerted forces CANNOT exist alone.

(h) The force of attraction exerted by the huge mass of the earth is called gravity. (11)
i.e. Gravity is a force of attraction.
Gravity is an example of a natural force. (13)
i.e. Gravity is a natural force.
∴ Gravity is a natural force and it is also a force of attraction.
It is NOT TRUE that natural forces (i.e. all natural forces) are forces of attraction.

(i)   When a force acts on a rigid body it is balanced by an equal reaction force which acts in the opposite direction. (16)

i.e.   When a force acts on a rigid body there is a reaction force of the same magnitude as the force which acts on the body.

∴   When a force acts on a rigid body the magnitude of the reaction force depends on the magnitude of the force acting on the body.
It is NOT TRUE that when a force acts on a rigid body the magnitude of the reaction force depends on the size of the rigid body.

(j)   If a man stands on a slippery surface and brings a force to bear on a heavy load, the reaction force makes him slide backwards. (17)

i.e.   He slides backwards because of a reaction force.
Similarly if a man fires a rifle, the force which pushes the bullet forwards will be matched by a force which makes the gun push backwards against his shoulder. (18)

i.e.   The gun pushes backwards because of a reaction force.

∴   *The force which pushes a gun backwards when it is fired is a reaction force.*

EXERCISE A *Rephrasing*

Rewrite the following, replacing the words printed in italics with expressions from the passage which have a similar meaning.

1. A heavy mass may *extend* a copper wire.
2. Newton investigated *the force of attraction exerted by the huge mass of the earth.*
3. The force which pushes a bullet forwards is *balanced* by a reaction force.
4. A force cannot exist *in isolation.*
5. Gravity is a *naturally exerted force.*
6. *Gravitational force* is a force of attraction.
7. When a *rifle* is fired it recoils.
8. When a force *is brought to bear* on a rigid body there is an equal but opposite reaction force.

EXERCISE B *Contextual reference*

1. In sentence 2, 'it' refers to
   (a) an effect
   (b) a force

2. In sentence 4, 'it' refers to
   (a) a force
   (b) a small object

3. In sentence 6, 'it' refers to
   (a) a moving car
   (b) a brake

4. In sentence 14, 'it' refers to
   (a) a force
   (b) a naturally exerted force

5. In sentence 16, 'it' refers to
   (a) a force
   (b) a rigid body

EXERCISE C *Relationships between statements*

Place the following expressions in the sentences indicated. Replace and re-order the words in the sentences where necessary.

on the other hand (5)	for example (13)
for example (6)	for this reason (16)
in addition (9)	a further example is that (18)
thus (12)	

II USE OF LANGUAGE

EXERCISE A *Instructions and results*

Copy the column of instructions below into your notebook. Then write down and complete each sentence in the results column using the information from the reading passage. Sentence 1 has been completed for you.

instruction	*result*
1. Push against a small object.	The object moves.
2. Brake a moving car.	The car . . . .
3. Suspend a heavy mass from a copper wire.	The wire . . . .
4. Release a heavy weight from a height of one metre.	The weight . . . .
5. Stand on slippery ground and push against a heavy load.	Our feet . . . .
6. Hold a gun against your shoulder and fire it.	The gun . . . .
7. Apply a force of 500 N to a thin metal rod.	The rod . . . .

| 8. Apply a force of 2 kN suddenly to an iron casting. | The casting . . . . |

9. Apply a load of 1 kN to the end of a steel upright.

The upright . . . .

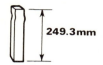

10. Apply a force to a rigid body. The force is balanced . . . .
11. Suspend a brick from a spring balance. The spring . . . .
12. Strike a piece of glass with a hammer. The glass . . . .

EXERCISE B *Making observations* (i)

When we state the result of following an instruction, we make an *observation*. Look at this example:

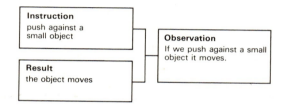

Now write observations like this from each of the instruction-result pairs in Exercise A.

EXERCISE C *Making observations* (ii)

We can write an observation in several different ways. Look at these examples:

(a) using *when*:   When we push against a small object it moves.

(b) putting the result first: A small object moves if we push against it.

(c) using the passive: If a small object is pushed against, it moves. A small object moves when it is pushed against.

Now rewrite each of the observations you made in Exercise B using pattern (a), (b) or (c).

EXERCISE D *Relative clauses (defining)*

Look at the following sentences:

(a) *Loads* cause tensile stresses.
(b) *The loads* tend to pull a body apart.

If the noun phrases in italics refer to the same thing, we can combine the two sentences into one by using a relative clause:

(c) Loads which tend to pull a body apart cause tensile stresses.

Write down a single sentence for each of the following pairs of sentences. Make the second sentence into a relative clause and insert it into the first sentence at the place marked by dots.

EXAMPLE

A lever . . . can be used to compare two masses.
Such a lever has the fulcrum placed between load and effort.
=   A lever which has the fulcrum placed between load and effort can be used to compare two masses.

1. A strut is a member . . .
   The member resists a compressive force.
2. The beams . . . are welded together.
   They form the chassis of the truck.
3. Rust may attack certain metals. . . .
   These metals contain some proportion of iron.
4. We can combine information on the size of a force and the distance it moves, in a diagram . . . .
   The diagram is called a work diagram.
5. Sir Isaac Newton put forward a law . . .
   The law states that every action has an equal and opposite reaction.

EXERCISE E *Relative clauses (non-defining)*

Compare the following sentences:

(a) The mill *which produces sheet steel* was made in Scotland but the mill *which produces tube steel* was made in Sweden.
(b) The mill, *which produces sheet steel,* was made in Scotland.

In sentence (a) the relative clauses tell us which mill we are talking about. In sentence (a) we have two *defining* relative clauses. In sentence (b) we already know which mill we are talking about. The clause simply adds some extra information about the mill. In sentence (b) we have a *non-defining* relative clause. Note the use of commas.

In Exercise D you made sentences with defining relative clauses. In this exercise, make the second sentence into a relative clause and insert it into the first sentence at the place marked by dots. You will write sentences with non-defining relative clauses.

EXAMPLE

Brass, . . . , is used to make bolts and screws.
Brass is an alloy of copper and zinc.
Brass, which is an alloy of copper and zinc, is used to make bolts and screws.

1. The rectangular block of steel, . . ., is fixed to the floor.
   The block measures 100 by 200 by 10 mm.
2. The electric motor, . . . , is linked to the driving shaft by a belt.
   The motor has a mass of 400 kg.
3. Polished steel, . . . , is in fact covered with tiny bumps.
   Polished steel is normally described as flat and smooth.
4. Friction, . . . , dissipates mechanical energy by converting it into heat energy.
   Friction is always present in a machine.
5. Stainless steel contains chromium, ...
   The chromium makes the steel corrosion-resistant.

EXERCISE F *Relative clauses* (*defining and non-defining*)

Now join the following pairs of sentences and state whether the completed sentences contain defining or non-defining relative clauses.

EXAMPLE
The micrometer screw gauge, . . . , consists of a steel frame carrying a sleeve on which a thimble turns.
The micrometer screw gauge is used by engineers to obtain very accurate measurements.
= The micrometer screw gauge, which is used by engineers to obtain very accurate measurements, consists of a steel frame carrying a sleeve on which a thimble turns. (non-defining)
1. The body is just on the point of sliding at the angle . . . .
   The angle is known as the angle of friction.
2. A railway engine, . . . , draws a train of eight coaches, each of mass 17 tonnes, up a gradient of 1 in 40.
   The engine has a mass of 80 tonnes.
3. The screw-jack is basically a screw running through a fixed nut . . . .
   The nut is incorporated in the jack.
4. As the cord is wound off the wheel, the load cord, . . . , is wound on and thus overcomes the load.
   The load cord is attached to the axle.
5. The gear . . . rotates in an opposite direction to the first.
   The gear is last in an even series of gears in mesh.
6. Intermediate gears, . . . , are often referred to as idlers.
   Intermediate gears do not affect the ratio of the gear train.
7. Hoisting winches of the first group, . . . , are termed single purchase crab winches.
   These winches employ a simple gear train.
8. This diagram means that the tensile force . . . must exceed 3 kN.
   The tensile force will cause permanent distortion.
9. Complicated mechanisms . . . are machines just as simple levers are machines.
   These complicated mechanisms make up an aeroplane engine.

10. Malleable cast iron, ... , is tougher than grey cast iron.
    Malleable cast iron is a ferrous metal.
11. Steels . . . are called tool steels.
    These steels are used to make tools.
12. The Kariba dam, . . . , provides electric power for Zambia.
    The dam is situated on the Zambesi.

EXERCISE G *Noun modification* (i)

If we want to describe an object in greater detail we may use an adjective:
    water – *hot* water
    metal – *ferrous* metal
    lever – *simple* lever
We can also put a noun in front of a noun:
    a cylinder – a *steel* cylinder
    a bearing – a *brass* bearing
    a filter – an *air* filter
Many grammatical relationships are possible in Noun+Noun constructions,
or *noun compounds*. Look at the following examples:

  (a) a diesel engine   =   an engine *which uses* diesel oil
  (b) a brass bearing   =   a bearing *which is made of* brass
  (c) carbon steel   =   steel *which contains* carbon
  (d) a capstan lathe   =   a lathe *which has* a capstan

Find further examples of each type in the following list. Mark each phrase
(a), (b), (c) or (d).

EXAMPLE
    phosphor bronze   (c)

air motor   electric drill
turret lathe   metal casting
chromium steel   concrete bridge
steel plate   heat engine
wing nut   aluminium alloy

What new relationships can you discover in the following list? Rewrite each
combination to show the relationship between the two nouns.

EXAMPLE
    a foot brake   =   a brake *which is operated by* foot

Wankel engine   test piece
heat treatment   water tube
force system   fuel gas
hand pump   instrument lathe
needle valve   gear lubricant
dockside crane   mushroom valve

SYMBOL	EXAMPLE	MEANING IN FULL
·	3·14159	three *point* one four one five nine
+	u+v	u *plus* v
−	v−u	v *minus* u
=	1 tonne = 1,000 kg	one tonne *is equal to* one thousand kilogrammes / *equals*
≠	x ≠ y	x *does not equal* y / *equals not*
×	mass × velocity	mass *multiplied by* velocity / *times*
no sign between two quantities	momentum = mv	momentum equals m *multiplied by* v / *times*
÷	8÷2	eight *divided by* two
one quantity over another	speed = $\dfrac{\text{distance}}{\text{time taken}}$	speed equals *the ratio of* distance *to* time taken / speed equals distance *divided by* time taken / *over*
/	20 km/h	twenty kilometres *per* hour
≡	1 mm vertical ≡ 5 N	one millimetre vertical *is equivalent to* five newtons
≃	60 km/h ≃ 17 m/s	sixty kilometres per hour *is approximately equal to* seventeen metres per second
∝	stress ∝ strain	stress *is proportional to* strain
:	2:1	two *to* one
%	0·4%	zero point four *per cent*
√⁻	$\sqrt{5}$	*the square root of* five / *root* five
2 3	2^2 3^3	two *squared* three *cubed*
4 − 5	10^4 10^{-5}	ten *to the power* four ten *to the power* *minus* five
>	>18 mm	*greater than* eighteen millimetres
<	<20 mm	*less than* twenty millimetres
≧ ≦	≧40 mm ≦100 mm	*greater than or equal to* forty millimetres *less than or equal to* one hundred millimetres
±	±2 kg	*plus or minus* two kilogrammes
°	90° 349°C	ninety *degrees* three hundred and forty-nine *degrees* Centigrade
′	6° 32′	six degrees thirty-two *minutes*

III INFORMATION TRANSFER

EXERCISE A *Mathematical symbols used in engineering*

Study the table on the opposite page. Now write out the following mathematical expressions in full:

1. force $\propto$ mass $\times$ acceleration
2. power $= \dfrac{\text{work done}}{\text{time taken}}$
3. 1 rad $\simeq 57 \cdot 3°$
4. efficiency $= \dfrac{\text{useful output}}{\text{input}} \times 100\%$
5. $\pm 0 \cdot 15$ mm on all dimensions
6. $6{,}820$ mm^2 $= 6{,}820 \times 10^{-6}$ m^2
7. air : petrol $= 15{:}1$
8. g $\simeq 9 \cdot 81$ m/s^2
9. 400 mm^2 area $\equiv 50$ J
10. power $=$ Fv

EXERCISE B *Greek letters and abbreviations used in engineering*

The following Greek letters are used in engineering:

α	alpha		μ	mu
β	beta		π	pi
γ	gamma	Σ	σ	sigma
δ	delta		τ	tau
ε	epsilon		ϕ	phi
η	eta		ω	omega
θ	theta			

The following abbreviations are used in the mathematics of engineering:

abbreviation	in full
sin	sine
cos	cosine
sec	secant
cosec	cosecant
tan	tangent
cot	cotangent

Now write out the following expressions in full:

1. $\tan \phi = \mu$
2. 1 radian $= \dfrac{180°}{\pi} \simeq 57 \cdot 3°$

3. power absorbed by brake $= \mu R \times 2\pi rnW$

4. average speed between P and Q $= \dfrac{\delta s}{\delta t}$

5. $R = \sqrt{[(\Sigma P_x)^2 + (\Sigma P_y)^2]}$

6. pitch $= 2h \tan \frac{1}{2}\phi$

7. efficiency $= \eta = \dfrac{M.A.}{V.R.}$

8. force required to hold the body at rest $= m_g \sin \theta N$

9. $V = \frac{1}{3}\pi r^3 \cot \alpha$

10. $\theta = \omega t + \frac{1}{2}\alpha t^2$

11. $b = \frac{1}{2}p \sec \frac{1}{2}\beta$

12. $\gamma = 26° \, 34'$

IV   GUIDED WRITING

STAGE 1 *Sentence building*

Join the following groups of sentences to make 12 longer sentences. Where a connecting word is given at the beginning of a group, use it to join the sentences. Where there is no connecting word, use a relative clause. Make any punctuation changes you think are necessary.

1. We can think of the weight of a body as acting at one point.
   This point is known as the body's centre of gravity.

2. ALTHOUGH
   A body will always act as if its mass were concentrated at its centre of gravity.
   Its centre of gravity need not be within the body itself.

3. SUCH AS
   The centre of gravity of some regular shapes can be found by inspection.
   A cube is a regular shape.

4. FOR EXAMPLE
   It is easy to make such regular shapes stand upright.
   A cylinder will stand on its base.

5. If a body is to stand upright, the line of action of its weight must act through the base.
   The line of action of its weight passes through its centre of gravity.

6. AND THEREFORE
   If a rectangular solid is placed on one face its weight will act through the centre of the base.
   The solid will stand upright.

7. BUT
   If the solid is tilted slightly, the line of action of its weight will move towards the edge of the base.
   It will still fall within the base.

8. THEREFORE
   If the solid is tilted further, the line drawn vertically downwards from its centre of gravity will fall outside the base.
   The solid will topple over.

9. WHEREAS
   If a body returns to its original position after a slight disturbance it is said to be stable.
   If a body moves into a new position after a slight disturbance it is said to be unstable.

10. BECAUSE
    Unstable structures can be dangerous.
    They have to be stabilized.

11. Cranes are normally stabilized by a large counter-weight.
    This counter-weight ensures that the total mass of the crane and its load always acts through the crane's base.

12. SO THAT
    Cranes often have a warning device which operates when the safe load is exceeded.
    The crane is never in danger of toppling over.

STAGE 2 *Paragraph building*

Now group the completed sentences into two paragraphs. You will have to add 'For example' at the beginning of sentence 6, 'For instance' at the beginning of sentence 11 and 'In addition' at the beginning of sentence 12. Give the passage the title 'Stability'.

STAGE 3 *Using diagrams to illustrate the passage*

Here are three sketches to illustrate the passage.

 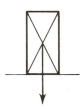 

Label the sketches Diagram 1, Diagram 2 and Diagram 3 and insert references to them in the completed passage. For example,

> See Diagram 2
> As in Diagram 1
> This is illustrated by Diagram 3

V   FREE READING

Read the following passage in your own time. If there are any words you do not know, look them up in your dictionary. Try to find additional examples of the points you have studied in this and other units.

GRAVITY

A force of attraction exists between every body in the universe. It has been investigated by many scientists including Galileo and Newton. This gravitational force depends on the mass of the bodies involved. Normally it is very small but when one of the bodies is a planet, like the earth, the force is considerable. Everything on or near the surface of the earth is attracted by the mass of the earth. The greater the mass, the greater is the earth's force of attraction on it. We call this force of attraction gravity.

Because of gravity, bodies have weight. We can perceive weight only when a body resists gravity. For example, when we pick up a stone there are two forces involved. One is the lifting force we exert and the other is the force of gravity which attracts the stone downwards and thus gives it weight. When a body escapes from the influence of the earth's gravitational pull, it can become 'weightless'. For example, the centrifugal force of a spacecraft spinning in orbit round the earth cancels the effect of gravity. The crew therefore experience weightlessness. One of the minor disadvantages of weightlessness is that normal pens will not write because the ink is not attracted by gravity to flow out of the pen.

If the space crew land on the surface of the moon, they experience the much weaker force of gravity exerted by the moon. On the moon they weigh less than on the earth. Special training is necessary to help them to walk on the moon's surface.

To simplify engineering calculations, it is assumed that gravity is the same everywhere on the earth's surface, and that for every kilogramme of mass the earth exerts a force of 9·81 newtons on a body. In fact gravity differs slightly from place to place because of the shape of the earth. It is greatest at the poles where the earth is flattest and is least at the Equator.

4 Friction

[1]Whenever one surface moves over another, a force is set up which resists the movement. [2]This force, which we call friction, always opposes motion. [3]It exists in every machine. [4]It can be reduced by lubrication but never completely removed. [5]In general, the force opposing motion is slightly greater before one surface starts moving over another surface than after movement has started. [6]This slightly greater force is called static friction. [7]The force which must be overcome to keep one surface moving over another is known as sliding friction. [8]Static friction is greater than sliding friction.

(a) Friction always occurs when there is movement between surfaces.
(b) We can remove all sliding friction by lubricating moving surfaces.
(c) To start a body moving requires a greater force than to keep it moving.
(d) Sliding friction opposes motion.
(e) Friction is a force.

[9]The value of sliding friction depends on the nature of the two surfaces which touch each other. [10]Thus friction between two rough planks can be lessened if they are made smooth. [11]Sliding friction is independent of the area of surface in contact. [12]In theory a small brake pad will exert as much braking force as a large one of greater surface area. [13]In practice a small pad will wear down more quickly and therefore is not used. [14]One other law of friction should be noted. [15]We can make the normal reaction between two surfaces in contact twice as large by doubling the mass carried by one surface. [16]If we do so we find that sliding friction between the surfaces is also doubled. [17]If we halve the mass carried, sliding friction is also halved. [18]This shows that sliding friction is proportional to the reaction between the surfaces in contact.

(f) When the area of surfaces in contact is increased, sliding friction between them is increased.

Large brake pads are used instead of small ones because they exert a greater braking force

(h) Sliding friction between rough planks is greater than between smooth planks.

(i) If the mass of a body sliding over another is increased, the sliding friction force between them will also increase.

(j) If we halve the area of surfaces in contact, we will halve the sliding friction between the surfaces.

Solutions

(a) Whenever one surface moves over another, a force is set up which resists the movement. (1)

whenever = always

i.e. When there is a movement between two surfaces a force is always set up. This force, which we call friction . . . . (2)

i.e. The force which is set up is called friction

∴ *Friction always occurs when there is movement between two surfaces.*

(b) It can be reduced by lubrication but never completely removed. (4)

i.e. Friction can be reduced by lubrication but never completely removed.

Friction (here) = static friction and sliding friction

i.e. We can reduce sliding friction by lubrication but we can never remove all sliding friction.

∴ We CANNOT remove all sliding friction by lubricating moving surfaces.

(c) In general, the force opposing motion is slightly greater before one surface starts moving over another surface than after movement has started. (5)

i.e. The force which must be overcome to start one surface moving over another is greater than the force which must be overcome to maintain movement.

∴ *To start a body moving requires a greater force than to keep it moving.*

(d) This force, which we call friction, always opposes motion. (2)

i.e. Friction opposes motion.

Friction (here) = static and sliding friction.

∴ *Sliding friction opposes motion.*

(e) This force, which we call friction, always opposes motion. (2)

i.e. *Friction is a force.*

(f) Sliding friction is independent of the area of surface in contact. (11)

i.e. Increasing the area of surfaces in contact will not increase the magnitude of sliding friction between the surfaces.

∴ It is NOT TRUE that when the area of surfaces in contact is increased, sliding friction between them is also increased.

(g) In theory a small brake pad will exert as much braking force as a large one of greater surface area. (12)

i.e. Theoretically, small brake pads will exert as much braking force as large ones.

but In practice a small pad will wear down more quickly and therefore is not used. (13)

i.e. Large pads are used in practice because they do not wear down so quickly.

∴ It is NOT TRUE that large brake pads are used instead of small ones because they exert a greater braking force.

(h) Thus friction between two rough planks can be lessened if they are made smooth. (10)

i.e. Friction must be greater when the planks are rough than when they are smooth.

Friction (here) = static and sliding friction

∴ *Sliding friction between rough planks is greater than between smooth planks.*

(i) This shows that sliding friction is proportional to the reaction between the surfaces in contact. (18)

i.e. If the reaction between the two surfaces in contact is increased, sliding friction is also increased.

but We can make the normal reaction between two surfaces in contact twice as large by doubling the mass carried by one surface. (15)

i.e. The reaction between surfaces in contact increases as the mass carried by one surface increases.

∴ *If the mass of a body sliding over another is increased, the sliding friction force between them will also increase.*

(j) Sliding friction is independent of the area of surface in contact. (11)

i.e. If we halve the area of surfaces in contact we will not affect sliding friction between them.

∴ If we halve the area of surfaces in contact we will NOT halve the sliding friction between the surfaces.

EXERCISE A *Rephrasing*

Rewrite the following, replacing the words printed in italics with expressions from the passage which have a similar meaning.
1. Friction always *resists* motion.
2. Friction can be *lessened* by oiling the moving surfaces.

3. *The force which must be overcome to keep one surface moving over another* is smaller than static friction.
4. Moving surfaces *which touch each other* must be lubricated.
5. If the areas in contact are *made twice as large* the force of sliding friction will remain the same.
6. Friction opposes *movement*.

EXERCISE B *Contextual reference*

1. In sentence 2, 'this force' refers to   (a) the force which resists the movement
                                        (b) the force which moves one surface over another
2. In sentence 3, 'it' refers to   (a) friction
                                        (b) motion
3. In sentence 4, 'it' refers to   (a) a machine
                                        (b) friction
4. In sentence 10, 'they' refers to   (a) the two surfaces
                                        (b) two rough planks
                                        (c) sliding and static friction
5. In sentence 12, 'one' refers to   (a) braking force
                                        (b) brake pad
                                        (c) a law of friction

EXERCISE C *Relationships between statements*

Place the following expressions in the sentences indicated. Replace and re-order the words in the sentences where necessary. Where two sentences are indicated, join them using the expression given.

on the other hand (7)   although (12+13)
whereas (6+7)   however (13)
in more general terms (8)   similarly (17)
for instance (10)   we can conclude (18)
therefore (12)

II USE OF LANGUAGE

EXERCISE A *Instructions and results*

Copy the column of instructions below in your notebook. Then write down and complete the results column using the information from the reading passage. Sentence 1 has been completed for you.

instruction	*result*
1. Place a smooth roller on an inclined plane.	The roller rolls down the plane.
2. Push a table across a rough floor.	A force is set up which . . . . motion.
3. Double the forces pressing two moving surfaces together.	Sliding friction between the two surfaces is . . . .
4. Lubricate two moving surfaces.	Sliding friction . . . .
5. Grease the surface of a shaft rotating in a bearing.	Sliding friction . . . .

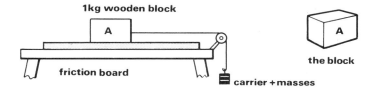

6. Measure the force required to start the block moving *and* measure the force required to keep the block moving.	We find that the force . . . . is greater than the force . . . .
7. Lay the block on side A and measure the force required to keep the block moving.	We find that the force . . . is . . . .
8. Add a 1 kg mass to the block and measure the force required to keep the block moving.	We find that the force . . . is . . . .
9. Substitute a glass sheet for the friction board and measure the force required to keep the block moving.	We find that the force required to keep the block moving . . . .

EXERCISE B *Making observations* (iii)

Combine the instructions and results in Exercise A to make observations (refer to Unit 3 Exercise C, p. 28).

EXERCISE C *Making inductions*

From one or more observations we can make a special kind of generalization called an *induction*. Look at the following example:

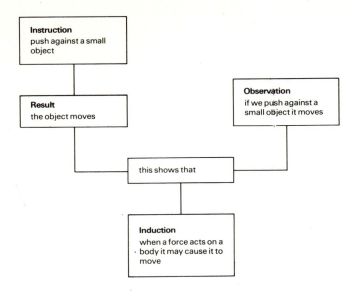

There are a number of generalizations in the reading passage which can act as inductions. You will find them in sentences 2, 4, 8, 9, 11 and 18. Make your own table as below and write these inductions in your column (b).

	a	b	
1.	....	Friction	(2)
	....	....	
2.	....	Friction	(4)
	....	.... by lubrication.	
3.	....	....	(8)
	....	....	
4.	....	....	(9)
	....	....	
5.	....	....	(11)
	....	....	
6.	....	Sliding friction	(18)
	....	....	

Now write in each space in column (a) of your table one of the observations which you made in Exercise B. Make sure that the inductions and the observations match. Then combine the observations and inductions.

EXAMPLE

If we push against a small object it moves. This shows that when a force acts on a body it may cause it to move.

EXERCISE D *Short-form relative clauses* (i)

We have seen (Unit 3) that if two sentences each contain a noun phrase, and the noun phrases refer to the same thing, then the sentences can be joined together by a relative pronoun like *which*.

EXAMPLE

The block is resting on a plane.
The plane is inclined at an angle of 30° to the horizontal.
= The block is resting on a plane *which is inclined at an angle of 30° to the horizontal.*

We can make this sentence shorter by omitting *which is*:

The block is resting on a plane *inclined at an angle of 30° to the horizontal.*

In the same way we can omit *which is* from the following sentence:

The plane *which is flying at an altitude of 2,140 metres* is subjected to pressures of 80 kilonewtons per square metre.
= The plane *flying at an altitude of 2,140 metres* is subjected to pressures of 80 kilonewtons per square metre.

Now join the following sentence pairs omitting *which* wherever possible. In each case indicate whether the relative clause is a defining or a non-defining clause.

1. Steels . . . are known as alloy steels.
   These steels are mixed with one or more metallic elements.
2. Tests . . . are of two kinds – tests to destruction and tests within the elastic limit.
   These tests are applied to materials.
3. The power developed by the generator . . . is 20 kW.
   The generator is revolving at 1,000 rev/min.
4. A dockside crane, . . . , has a safe working load of 3×10^3 kg.
   The crane is mounted on a set of rails.
5. The distance . . . is plotted on a graph against time taken.
   The distance is travelled by a moving load.
6. These forces constitute a tensile stress, . . . , which acts around the circumference of the cylinder.
   This stress is known as hoop stress.
7. The force . . . was found to be 1,200 N.
   The force was exerted on the clamps.
8. Bridges, roof trusses and cranes are structures . . . .
   Such structures are designed to resist forces.

EXERCISE E: *Short-form relative clauses* (ii)

Look at this example:
    The steel beams are welded together.
    The beams form the chassis of the truck.

We can join these two sentences in two ways:
     (a) The steel beams *which form the chassis of the truck* are welded together.
or (b) The steel beams *forming the chassis of the truck* are welded together.

In sentence (b) we have made the relative clause shorter by omitting *which* and changing the verb to its *-ing* form. What kind of relative clause does sentence (a) contain – defining or non-defining?

If the relative clause contains *which*+a verb in the simple present we can omit *which* and change the verb to its *-ing* form. This rule can be applied if

    (a) the clause is a defining one
or (b) the verb is a verb of state

Verbs of state describe states not actions like 'work' or 'run'. The most common verbs of state in engineering are

measure	contain
weigh	hold
consist	form

Now join the following sentence pairs omitting *which* wherever possible. In each case indicate whether the relative clause is defining or non-defining and underline verbs of state.

1. XY is a steel shaft . . . .
   It carries a 300 mm diameter eccentric gear.
2. A flywheel, . . . , has a diameter of 1·6 m.
   The flywheel consists of a cast iron rim which is connected to a boss by spokes.
3. The driving belt, . . . , is 9 mm thick.
   It transmits power to the pulleys.
4. The towers, . . . , support the main section of the bridge.
   The towers weigh a thousand tonnes each.
5. The tapping head has a spring clutch, ...
   The clutch allows the tap to slip without breaking when the load becomes excessive.
6. Grooving tools, . . . , are made of high-speed steel.
   Grooving tools cut slots or keyways.
7. The main shaft of the lathe drives the lubricant pump, ...
   The pump supplies cooling fluid at the tool cutting tip.

8. Bronze . . . is called phosphor bronze.
   This bronze contains 0·8 % phosphorus.

EXERCISE F *Short-form relative clauses* (iii)

When the relative clause contains *which+have* we can shorten it in two
ways. Look at the following examples:

> Two steel sheets *which have a thickness of 3 mm each* are joined by
> rivets.
> = (a) Two steel sheets *having a thickness of 3 mm each* are joined by rivets.
> *or* (b) Two steel sheets *with a thickness of 3 mm each* are joined by rivets.

Now join these sentence pairs and omit *which* where possible:

1. Grey cast iron is a soft close-grained cast iron . . . .
   This cast iron has a relatively low melting point.
2. A diesel engine . . . is called a slow-speed diesel.
   This engine has a running speed of 75 to 250 rev/min.
3. A dockside crane . . . is mounted on a set of rails.
   The crane has a safe working load of 2,000 kg.
4. A milling machine . . . is known as a universal milling machine.
   This machine has a swivelling table.

EXERCISE G *Noun modification* (ii)

In Unit 3 we studied a number of noun compounds. Another common way
of modifying a noun can be seen in the following example:

> The load is distributed uniformly.
> = It is a uniformly distributed load.

Now rewrite the following sentences in the same way:

1. The load was applied suddenly.
2. The forces are perfectly matched.
3. The bar is fixed rigidly.
4. The material corrodes easily.
5. The surface treatment was developed recently.
6. The crane hook is stressed heavily.
7. The salt bath furnace is heated externally.
8. The force was exerted deliberately.
9. We work the forging plastically.
10. The tool drum is controlled automatically.

III INFORMATION TRANSFER

EXERCISE A *Making recommendations based on a graph*

Study the following graph, which shows recommended speeds for carbon steel drills on soft steel:

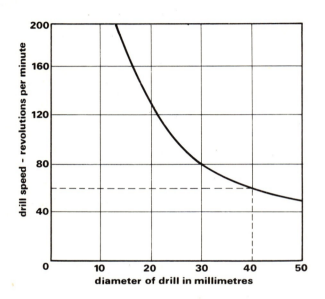

When we make recommendations we use *should* or *ought to*.

EXAMPLE
  For 40 mm drills a speed of 60 rev/min *should* be used.
  For 40 mm drills a speed of 60 rev/min *ought to* be used.

Now, using the graph, write similar sentences giving the recommended speeds for drills of the following diameters.

1. 20 mm	4. 12·5 mm
2. 25 mm	5. 30 mm
3. 50 mm	6. 15 mm

EXERCISE B *Making recommendations based on a table*

The table opposite shows recommended shaft limits for ball bearings of different bores:

Bearing bore mm	Shaft limits mm	
	Heavy loading	Light loading
−12	—	+0·003 −0·005
12·1−30	—	+0·005 −0·003
30·1−50	—	+0·007 −0·003
50·1−75	+0·018 −0·003	+0·013 −0·000
75·1−100	+0·023 −0·005	+0·016 −0·003
100·1−120	+0·028 −0·010	+0·020 −0·005

We can use this table to write recommendations.

EXAMPLES

The shaft limits for a ball bearing of 15 mm bore *should be* 15·005 mm and 14·997 mm.

The shaft limits for a ball bearing of 80 mm bore *ought to be* 80·023 mm and 79·995 mm for a heavily loaded shaft and 80·016 mm and 79·997 mm for a lightly loaded shaft.

Now write similar sentences giving the recommended shaft limits for the following:

1. a bearing of 10 mm bore
2. a bearing of 30 mm bore
3. a bearing of 60 mm bore for a lightly loaded shaft
4. a bearing of 110 mm bore for a heavily loaded shaft
5. a bearing of 65 mm bore for both a heavily loaded and a lightly loaded shaft

IV   GUIDED WRITING

STAGE 1 *Sentence and paragraph building*

Join the following groups of sentences to make eight longer sentences. You are given some, but not all, of the connecting words which you will need. You may omit or change words where you think it is necessary, and you should provide appropriate punctuation. When you have finished, the eight sentences should make a logical paragraph.

1. ALTHOUGH/WHEN
   The surface of a block of polished steel may seem perfectly flat.
   We examine the surface with a powerful microscope.
   We see that the surface is covered with tiny 'hills and valleys'.

2. IF
   We bring two steel surfaces together.
   The surfaces will touch at only a few points.
   These points are where one set of 'hills' meets another set.

3. BECAUSE/SO . . . THAT
   The total mass of the steel is concentrated at these points.
   The pressure on the points is great.
   The pressure causes the points of contact to weld together.

4. We apply a force to make one block of steel move over another block.
   We must first break the tiny welds.
   The blocks will move.

5. FOR THIS REASON
   To start a surface moving over another surface requires a force.
   This force is greater than the force required to keep the surfaces in motion.

6. The greater force represents static friction.
   The smaller force represents sliding friction.

7. One block slides over another.
   The two surfaces scrape against each other.
   This breaks off tiny pieces from each surface.

8. HOWEVER, IF
   We lubricate the two surfaces.
   Oil fills the tiny valleys.
   The surfaces do not weld together.
   One block can move over the other.

Now turn to the Free Reading passage and compare the paragraph you have written with the second paragraph in that passage.

V FREE READING

Read the following passage in your own time. If there are any words you do not know, look them up in your dictionary. Try to find additional examples of the points you have studied in this and other units.

LUBRICATION

Friction can be useful. For example, the screw-jack depends on friction between the body of the screw and the jack to prevent it running back under heavy loads. Belt drives depend on friction to prevent slipping. Brakes and vices are further examples of useful applications of friction. On the other hand, friction in machines causes loss of power. Twenty per cent of the power of a motor car is wasted in overcoming friction. Engineers try therefore to reduce friction as much as possible by good design. They can also use materials with a low coefficient of friction for devices such as bearings. The third method used for reducing friction is lubrication.

Although the surface of a block of polished steel may seem perfectly flat, when we examine it through a powerful microscope we see that it is covered with tiny 'hills and valleys'. If we bring two steel surfaces together they will touch at only a few points where one set of 'hills' meets another set. Because the total mass of the steel is concentrated at these points, the pressure on them is so great that it causes the points of contact to weld together. When we apply a force to make one block of steel move over another, we must first break these tiny welds before the blocks will move. For this reason, to start a surface moving over another surface requires a force greater than that required to keep the surfaces in motion. This greater force represents static friction whereas the smaller force represents sliding friction. When one block slides over another the two surfaces scrape against each other, breaking off tiny pieces from each surface. However, if we lubricate the two surfaces, oil fills the tiny valleys so that the surfaces do not weld together, and one block can move over the other.

Lubrication, then, reduces friction and because the surfaces do not scrape against each other it reduces wear on the material. Although dry friction can be eliminated in this way, some power will still be lost depending on the thickness of the lubricant used. Thus if the oil is too thick the lubricant itself will offer some resistance to motion. Selection of the correct lubricant depends on many factors, chief among which are the operating speeds of the machinery which is lubricated and the temperature range within which the machine must operate.

5 Levers

I   READING AND COMPREHENSION

[1]When a force acts on a body it may cause it to move in a straight line or to turn about a point or to do both. [2]A force can make a body rotate around a point which is not in its line of action. [3]If we push against the handle side of a door it will turn on its hinge and open. [4]The size of the turning effect of a force depends on the magnitude of the force and the perpendicular distance between its line of action and the point about which the body turns. [5]We call this point the fulcrum. [6]The turning effect of a force about a fulcrum is known as the moment of the force. [7]It is the product of the force and the distance at right angles between its line of action and its fulcrum.

(a)   A hinge is a fulcrum.
(b)   A force may make a body rotate about a point and move in a straight line at the same time.
(c)   The greater the perpendicular distance between a point and the line of action of a force, the greater the turning effect of the force about that point.
(d)   If we multiply length y by force F, we will obtain the moment of the force about point P

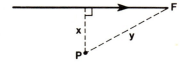

(e)   The moment of a force $= \dfrac{\text{force}}{\text{perpendicular distance between line of action and fulcrum}}$

[8]The lever is one application of the principle of the moment of a force about a point. [9]The lever is a simple machine. [10]An example is the crowbar, which is used to move large loads by means of smaller efforts. [11]Diagram 1

shows a crowbar being used to lift a heavy block. [12]The mass of the block is the load, the heel of the crowbar is the fulcrum and the force exerted by the man pressing down at X is the effort. [13]In the diagram a and b represent respectively the perpendicular distance between the effort and the fulcrum and the perpendicular distance between the load and the fulcrum. [14]By the principle of moments we can say that the man will just balance the load when

$$\text{effort} \times a = \text{load} \times b$$

[15]Any increase in the effort will raise the load further and may eventually cause it to overbalance.

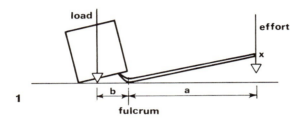

(f) The lever is the only application of the principle of the moment of a force about a point.

(g) The crowbar is a simple machine.

(h) Simple machines can use small efforts to move larger loads.

[16]Levers can be divided into three groups or orders. [17]They are classified according to the relative positions of the load, the effort and the fulcrum. [18]The positions are as follows:

first order: fulcrum between load and effort
second order: load between fulcrum and effort
third order: effort between fulcrum and load.

(i) A crowbar is a lever of the first order.

(j) With a crowbar, effort and load move in the same direction.

(k) All levers belong to a particular order.

(l) This diagram represents a third-order lever.

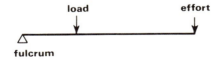

Solutions

(a) If we push against the handle side of a door it will turn on its hinge and open. (3)

i.e. The hinge is the point about which the door turns.

but . . . the point about which the body turns. (4) We call this point the fulcrum. (5)

i.e.   The point about which a body turns is a fulcrum.

∴   *A hinge is a fulcrum.*

(b)   When a force acts on a body it may cause it to move in a straight line or to turn about a point or to do both. (1)

i.e.   A force may make a body   (i) move in a straight line
                                   (ii) turn about a point
                                   (iii) move in a straight line and turn about
                                        a point

turn = rotate

∴   *A force may make a body rotate about a point and move in a straight line at the same time.*

(c)   It is the product of the force and the distance at right angles between its line of action and its fulcrum. (7)

It = the turning effect of a force
the distance at right angles = the perpendicular distance
fulcrum = the point about which a body turns

i.e.   The turning effect of a force is the product of the force and the perpendicular distance between its line of action and the point about which it turns.

∴   *The greater the perpendicular distance between a point and the line of action of a force, the greater the turning effect of the force about that point.*

(d)   It is the product of the force and the distance at right angles between its line of action and its fulcrum. (7)

It = the moment of a force
Point P is the fulcrum of force F.
Length x is the distance at right angles between the line of action of force F and point P.

i.e.   The moment of force F about point P is x times F.

∴   If we multiply length y by force F we will NOT obtain the moment of the force about point P.

(e)   It is the product of the force and the distance at right angles between its line of action and its fulcrum. (7)

It = the moment of a force

i.e.   The moment of a force is equal to the force multiplied by the perpendicular distance between its line of action and its fulcrum.

∴   The moment of a force is NOT equal to the force divided by the perpendicular distance between its line of action and its fulcrum.

(f)   The lever is one application of the principle of the moment of a force about a point. (8)

one ≠ the only

∴ It is NOT TRUE that the lever is the only application of the principle of the moment of a force about a point.

(g) The lever is a simple machine. (9) An example is the crowbar, which is used to move large loads by means of smaller efforts. (10)

i.e. The crowbar is an example of a simple machine which is a lever.

∴ *The crowbar is a simple machine.*

(h) An example is the crowbar, which is used to move large loads by means of smaller efforts. (10)

but The crowbar is a simple machine.

∴ *Simple machines can use small efforts to move larger loads.*

(i) *first order:* fulcrum between load and effort (18)
Diagram 1 shows that the crowbar has its fulcrum between the load and the effort.

∴ *A crowbar is a lever of the first order.*

(j) Look at diagram 1.
An effort pressing down at X will raise the load.

i.e. Effort and load move in opposite directions.

∴ With a crowbar, effort and load do NOT move in the same direction.

(k) Levers can be divided into three groups or orders. (16)

= Every lever is either a first-, second- or third-order lever.

∴ *All levers belong to a particular order.*

(l) *third order:* effort between fulcrum and load (18)
This diagram shows load between effort and fulcrum.

i.e. This diagram represents a second-order lever.

∴ This diagram does NOT represent a third-order lever.

EXERCISE A *Rephrasing*

Rewrite the following, replacing the words printed in italics with expressions from the passage which have a similar meaning.
1. A force may cause a body to *turn* about a point.
2. The crowbar will *cause* the load *to* overbalance.
3. The moment of a force is the product of the force and the perpendicular distance between its line of action and *the point about which the body turns*.
4. We measure the *perpendicular distance* between the force's line of action and its fulcrum.
5. *The moment of a force* is a vector quantity.
6. Levers are used to *lift* heavy blocks.
7. Levers may be *divided* into members of the first, second and third orders.

EXERCISE B *Contextual reference*

1. In sentence 3, 'it' refers to
   - (a) a handle
   - (b) a door

2. In sentence 4, 'its' refers to
   - (a) the force's
   - (b) the turning effect's

3. In sentence 5, 'this point' refers to
   - (a) the point about which the body turns
   - (b) the line of action of the force

4. In sentence 7, 'it' refers to
   - (a) the moment of a force
   - (b) the fulcrum
   - (c) the magnitude of the force

5. In sentence 15, 'it' refers to
   - (a) the effort
   - (b) the crowbar
   - (c) the load

6. In sentence 17, 'they' refers to
   - (a) load, effort and fulcrum
   - (b) three orders
   - (c) levers

EXERCISE C *Relationships between statements*

Place the following expressions in the sentences indicated. Replace and re-order the words in the sentences where necessary.

this means that (2)   since (14+15)
thus (2)   it follows that (15)
for example (3)

II   USE OF LANGUAGE

EXERCISE A *Completing a diagram*

Copy out the table opposite and fill in the spaces in parts 1 and 2, using the information from the reading passage.

EXERCISE B *Interpretation of diagrams*

Look at the drawings underneath the table opposite. Decide which kind of lever each drawing represents. Then fill in part 3 of your table, listing as many examples as you can.

EXERCISE C *Paragraphs based on diagrams*

Now use your completed table to write paragraphs.

EXAMPLE

Levers which have the fulcrum placed between load and effort are known as first-order levers. A crowbar is an example of a first-order lever.

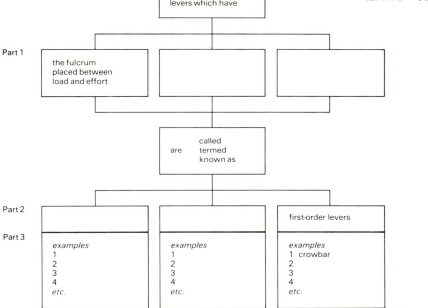

Part 1

levers which have

| the fulcrum placed between load and effort | | |

| are | called termed known as |

Part 2

Part 3

		first-order levers
examples 1 2 3 4 *etc.*	*examples* 1 2 3 4 *etc.*	*examples* 1 crowbar 2 3 4 *etc.*

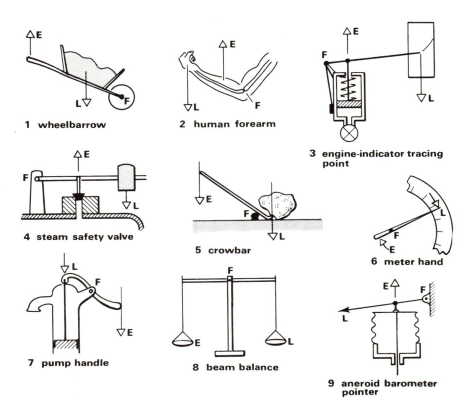

1 wheelbarrow

2 human forearm

3 engine-indicator tracing point

4 steam safety valve

5 crowbar

6 meter hand

7 pump handle

8 beam balance

9 aneroid barometer pointer

EXERCISE D *Describing the function of an object*

1. Study the following diagram:

2. Write as many sentences as you can based on the diagram.

EXAMPLE
   A third-order lever may be used to magnify a movement.

3. The sentences you made from the diagram describe the function of the different kinds of levers. We can describe the function of an object in three ways:
   (a) A third-order lever may be *used to magnify* a movement.
   (b) A third-order lever may be *used for magnifying* a movement.
   (c) A third-order lever may be *used as a means of magnifying* a movement.
   Now rewrite the sentences you made in section 2, using pattern (b) or (c).

4. Look back at the drawings on page 55. Decide in which way each lever is used and write a sentence for each drawing.

EXAMPLE
   A crowbar is an example of a first-order lever *used as a means of moving a large force with a smaller force.*

EXERCISE E *Combining sentences with an* -ing *clause*

Look at the following sentences:

(a) Belt drives are not so positive as gear drives.
(b) Belts tend to slip on high loads.

These can be combined into one sentence:

(c) Belt drives are not so positive as gear drives, belts tending to slip on high loads.

Combine each of the following pairs of sentences into one sentence by using an -*ing* clause in the same way:

1. A chain drive is similar to a belt drive except that the chain passes over sprockets on the chain wheel.
   This arrangement ensures that no slip takes place.
2. When a resultant force acts on a body an acceleration is produced.
   Its value depends on the mass of the body.
3. The length of the steel increases in proportion to the forces applied.
   Its cross-sectional area is unchanged.
4. The screw-jack is a screw revolving in a fixed nut.
   The screw thread provides a means of converting circular motion to motion in a straight line.
5. Work done by a force can be represented by a work diagram in the form of a graph.
   The vertical axis represents the force and the horizontal axis the distance moved.
6. The wheelbarrow is an example of a second-order lever.
   The load is carried between the fulcrum and the effort.
7. When a force is applied to the edge of a door it will turn.
   The hinge forms a fulcrum for the door.
8. Pressure is measured in newtons per square metre.
   The word 'per' implies that the force in newtons is divided by the area in square metres.
9. A crowbar is a first-order lever.
   The fulcrum is the heel of the crowbar.
10. The human forearm is a lever.
    The effort is provided by the muscle joining the upper arm to the forearm.

EXERCISE F *Relative clauses with prepositions*

In books about engineering we find many relative clauses with a preposition before *which*. Such clauses are formed in the following way:

> The shaft runs in brass bushes.
> The pulley is mounted *on the shaft*.
> = The shaft *on which* the pulley is mounted runs in brass bushes.

Combine each of the following pairs of sentences into one sentence containing a relative clause beginning with a preposition+*which*:

1. The main bearings consist of steel shells lined with aluminium.
   The shaft runs in the bearings.
2. The point is called the fulcrum.
   The body is free to rotate about the point.
3. The piers resist the load by a reaction of 5,000 N each.
   The bridge rests on the piers.
4. The points are 600 mm apart.
   The one kilogramme masses are suspended from the points.

5. The position of the arms of the lever will depend on the angle.
   The forces are required to act at the angle.
6. The rope passes over one pulley in the upper block.
   The lower block is attached to the rope.
7. The distance is double the displacement of the load.
   The effort moves through the distance.
8. Since earliest times man has tried to devise methods.
   A small effort can move a large load by the methods.
9. The efficiency of most machines rises quickly to reach a maximum value near those loads.
   The machine is designed for those loads.
10. A gear box is a unit.
   A compound gear train which can be altered by engaging different gears is housed in this unit.

EXERCISE G *Noun modification* (iii)

Some Noun+Noun combinations used in engineering contain a noun formed from a verb. Often the verb indicates the function of the object described.

EXAMPLE
   object: air-compressor
   function: to compress air

We can.express this information in a sentence:

   An air-compressor is used to compress air.

Write similar sentences to indicate the function of the following objects. Note that some of the nouns end in *-er* and some in *-or*.

speed governor	oil cooler
mass carrier	pressure regulator
casing liner	steam condenser
gas generator	shock absorber
air heater	hardness tester

What are the names of the following objects? Check the spelling in your dictionary.
   a device used to reduce the speed (of a motor)
   a device used to indicate the level of oil (in a gear box)
   a device used to grind the surface (of a metal plate)
   a device used to inject fuel (into petrol or diesel engines)
   a device used to filter oil (for an engine)
The information given in brackets does not form part of the name of the object.

III INFORMATION TRANSFER

EXERCISE A *Making comparisons based on a diagram*

Study the following diagram. Then read the comparison of mild steel and low carbon steel which is based on the information contained in the diagram.

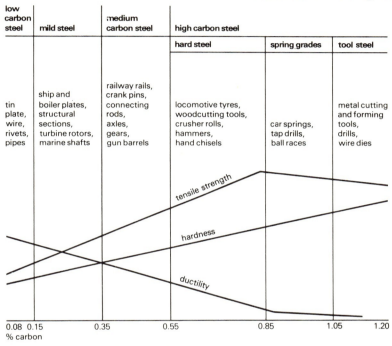

low carbon steel	mild steel	medium carbon steel	high carbon steel			
				hard steel	spring grades	tool steel
tin plate, wire, rivets, pipes	ship and boiler plates, structural sections, turbine rotors, marine shafts	railway rails, crank pins, connecting rods, axles, gears, gun barrels		locomotive tyres, woodcutting tools, crusher rolls, hammers, hand chisels	car springs, tap drills, ball races	metal cutting and forming tools, drills, wire dies

tensile strength

hardness

ductility

0.08 0.15   0.35   0.55   0.85   1.05   1.20
% carbon

Properties and applications of carbon steels

Low carbon steel contains between 0·08 and 0·15% carbon whereas mild steel contains between 0·15% and 0·35% carbon. Mild steel is stronger and harder than low carbon steel but it is less ductile. Low carbon steel is used to make tin plate, wire, rivets and pipes while mild steel is used for structural sections, turbine rotors, marine shafts and for ship and boiler plates.

Now write out and complete the following comparison of high and medium carbon steels using the information in the diagram.

High carbon steel contains between . . . and . . . carbon whereas medium carbon steel . . . . High carbon steel is . . . and . . . than . . . steel, but its strength . . . slightly when its carbon content is . . . than 0·83%. In addition . . . steel is less . . . than . . . steel. Medium carbon steel is used for . . . . High carbon steel with a . . . content up to . . . is used to make woodcutting tools, ... Car springs . . . are made from . . . with between . . . and . . . while metal cutting . . . are made from . . . with between . . . and . . . .

IV GUIDED WRITING

STAGE 1 *Writing a report of an experiment*

Here are a set of instructions for a simple experiment. Change the instructions into a report of the experiment as in the first example, and write the report in your notebook.

instructions	*report*
1. Pivot a metre stick at its centre point O so that it balances.	1. A metre stick was pivoted at its centre point O so that it balanced.
2. Attach a cord to a 1 kg mass and suspend it from a point P on the side OX, 200 mm from the centre point.	2. . . . .
3. Note what happens (the metre stick turns in an anti-clockwise direction).	3. It was noted that . . . .
4. Suspend a second mass of 1 kg mass from a point on the side OY.	4. . . . .
5. Adjust the distance between O and the mass until the stick remains in a horizontal position.	5. . . . .
6. Measure the distance between O and the second mass.	6. . . . . and was found to be 200 mm.
7. Replace the second 1 kg mass with a 0·5 kg mass.	7.
8. Note what happens (the metre stick turns anti-clockwise).	8. It was noted that . . . .
9. Move the 0·5 kg mass along OY until the stick again balances.	9. . . . .
10. Measure the distance between O and the point S where the 0·5 kg mass is suspended.	10. . . . . and was found to be 400 mm.

STAGE 2 *Illustrating the report with a diagram*

The following is a list of the apparatus which was used in the experiment.

a metre stick with a hole at its centre
a stand
pieces of cord
one 0·5 kg mass
two 1 kg masses

Refer to the list and draw a diagram to illustrate the experiment. Label the points O, P, S, X and Y. Label the other point mentioned in the report and mark it in the diagram.

STAGE 3 *Completing the report*

State the aim of the experiment and write down the two conclusions to complete the report. If you have difficulty you will find the two conclusions in the reading passage.

conclusions

    (i) The turning effect of a force depends on . . . .
    (ii) The turning effect of a force depends on . . . .

V   FREE READING

Read the following passage in your own time. If there are any words you do not know, look them up in your dictionary. Try to find additional examples of the points you have studied in this and other units.

BEAMS

When choosing a beam it is important to know its bending strength. The bending strength of the beam is the beam's resistance to bending moments. Diagram 1 shows a beam supported at both ends and carrying a load at its mid-point. The load makes the beam bend slightly. If we imagine the beam to consist of a number of longitudinal layers we can see that the top layer will be compressed by the load, and the bottom layer will be stretched as the beam bends. At the centre there will be a neutral layer which is neither stretched nor compressed.

    The beam is subjected to bending moments because the reaction at the supports causes clockwise and anti-clockwise moments as shown in the sketch. If the beam fails, the top layers will be crushed and the bottom layers torn. This failure will occur at mid-span where the bending moment is greatest.

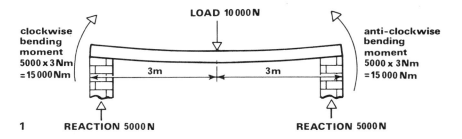

LOAD 10 000 N

clockwise bending moment 5000 x 3 Nm = 15 000 Nm

anti-clockwise bending moment 5000 x 3 Nm = 15 000 Nm

3m   3m

1   REACTION 5000 N   REACTION 5000 N

As most of the stress occurs at the top and bottom of a beam most of the material is concentrated at the top and bottom in the flanges. Material at the neutral layer is wasted as far as bending strength is concerned. In some girders, therefore, material is removed from the web. Diagram 2 shows a castellated girder, which is made by cutting a girder in two as shown, then reversing the ends and welding the two halves together. The result is a stronger beam for equal amounts of steel.

2

The depth of a beam is important in deciding what the resisting moment of the beam will be. The resisting moment of a beam resists the bending moment which tries to destroy the beam. The force produced by the tension of the top layers and the force produced by the compression of the bottom layers form a couple across the depth of the beam to provide a resisting moment. The deeper the beam, the longer the lever arm of the couple and hence the greater the resisting moment. In fact the beam's bending strength increases proportionally to the cube of the depth.

The reasons for the shape of the familiar I-section rolled steel beam now become clear. The flanges contain a lot of steel to resist compression and tension. The web of the beam is thin because it is not subjected to these stresses. The beam is deep compared to its width because its depth gives it a greater moment of resistance to offset bending moments.

6 Stress and Strain

I READING AND COMPREHENSION

[1]A body is in stress when forces are applied to it which cause its size and shape to change. [2]In other words, stress causes distortion. [3]The intensity of stress depends on the size of the force and the cross-sectional area (c.s.a.) of the body which resists the force. [4]That is,

$$\text{stress} = \frac{\text{applied force}}{\text{c.s.a. of the body}}$$

[5]Distortion due to stress is called strain. [6]Different forces will distort bodies in different ways. [7]A tensile force will lengthen a body. [8]One subjected to a compressive force will contract. [9]If a body has a uniform c.s.a., that is, if it has the same c.s.a. throughout its length, we calculate strain as

$$\text{strain} = \frac{\text{change of length}}{\text{original length}}$$

(a) Stress on bar x is greater than stress on bar y

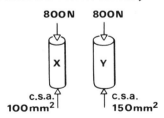

800N   **800N**

X   **Y**

c.s.a.
100mm^2   c.s.a.
150mm^2

(b) A tensile force can cause distortion.

(c) For this bar of steel, strain is equal to $\dfrac{1{,}000{\cdot}4}{1{,}000}$

Original length   **1000 mm**

New length   **1000·4 mm**
10kN ⟵ ═══════ ⟶ **10kN**

(d) Tensile forces and compressive forces have opposite effects on bodies.
(e) Distortion causes strain.

[10]Most materials used in engineering are elastic. [11]A material which has the property of elasticity will return to its original size and shape when the forces producing strain are removed. [12]However, if these forces go beyond a certain limit, called the elastic limit, an elastic material will not regain its original dimensions. [13]If we take a bar of uniform c.s.a. of an elastic material like mild steel, and apply gradually increasing tensile forces to it, it will extend. [14]If we measure each extension produced by each increase in force, we will find that the bar's increase in length is in proportion to the increase in force. [15]In other words, strain is proportional to stress. [16]A graph of stress against strain would therefore be a straight line like that in Diagram 1:

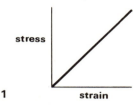

1

[17]Another way of expressing this is:

$$\frac{\text{stress}}{\text{strain}} = \text{a constant}$$

[18]The value of this constant is different for each elastic material. [19]It is called the Modulus of Elasticity. [20]If we exceed the elastic limit, then strain is no longer proportional to stress and there is permanent deformation. [21]These findings illustrate Hooke's law which states that within the elastic limit, the strain produced is proportional to the stress producing it.

(f) All engineering materials are elastic.
(g) Mild steel is an elastic material.
(h) Elastic materials cannot be in a state of stress.
(i) A mild steel bar will always extend in proportion to the forces which extend it.
(j) Within the elastic limit, if we double the stress on a body we will double the strain produced.
(k) The value of the Modulus of Elasticity varies according to the stress an elastic material is subjected to.
(l) Mild steel has a uniform c.s.a.

Solutions

(a) stress $= \dfrac{\text{applied force}}{\text{c.s.a. of the body}}$ (4)

i.e. stress on bar $x = \dfrac{800}{100} \text{N/mm}^2$ and stress on bar $y = \dfrac{800}{150} \text{N/mm}^2$

∴   *Stress on bar x is greater than stress on bar y.*

(b) A tensile force will lengthen a body. (7)

i.e. A tensile force will change the size and shape of a body.

∴ *A tensile force can cause distortion.*

(c) strain $= \dfrac{\text{change of length}}{\text{original length}}$ (9)

For this bar of steel, original length = 1,000 mm.

new length = 1,000·4 mm.

∴ change of length = 0·4 mm

∴ For this bar of steel, strain $= \dfrac{0·4}{1,000}$ NOT $\dfrac{1,000·4}{1,000}$

(d) A tensile force will lengthen a body. (7)

i.e. A tensile force will make a body longer.

One subjected to a compressive force will contract. (8)

i.e. A compressive force will make a body shorter.

∴ *Tensile forces and compressive forces have opposite effects on bodies.*

(e) Stress causes distortion. (2)

Distortion due to stress is called strain. (5)

i.e. stress causes distortion and this distortion is called strain

∴ It is NOT TRUE that distortion causes strain.

(f) Most materials used in engineering are elastic. (10)

most ≠ all

∴ It is NOT TRUE that all engineering materials are elastic.

(g) If we take a bar of uniform c.s.a. of an elastic material like mild steel, ... (13)

i.e. mild steel is an example of an elastic material

∴ *Mild steel is an elastic material.*

(h) If we take a bar of uniform c.s.a. of an elastic material like mild steel, and apply gradually increasing tensile forces to it, it will extend. (13)

i.e. If a tensile force is applied to an elastic material, it will extend.

= If a tensile force is applied to an elastic material, its size and shape will change.

∴ Elastic materials CAN be in a state of stress.

(i) If we measure each extension produced by each increase in force, we will find that the bar's increase in length is in proportion to the increase in force. (14)

i.e. The mild steel bar extends in proportion to the forces which extend it.

but If we exceed the elastic limit, then strain is no longer proportional to stress and there is permanent deformation. (20)

i.e. A mild steel bar will extend in proportion to the forces which extend it so long as those forces do not exceed the elastic limit for mild steel.

∴   It is NOT TRUE that a mild steel bar will always extend in proportion to the forces which extend it.

(j) Within the elastic limit, the strain produced is proportional to the stress producing it. (21)

i.e. Within the elastic limit, stress is proportional to strain.

∴   *Within the elastic limit, if we double the stress on a body we will double the strain produced.*

(k) The value of this constant is different for each elastic material. (18) It is called the Modulus of Elasticity. (19)

i.e. the Modulus of Elasticity is a constant

∴   The value of the Modulus of Elasticity does NOT vary according to the stress as elastic material is subjected to

(l) If we take a bar of uniform c.s.a. of an elastic material like mild steel, . . . (13)

i.e. The bar has a uniform c.s.a., not the steel. Only a shape can have a c.s.a. Mild steel can have many different shapes with different c.s.a.'s.

∴   It is NOT TRUE that mild steel has a uniform c.s.a.

EXERCISE A *Rephrasing*

Rewrite the following, replacing the words in italics with an expression from the text which has a similar meaning.

1. A tensile force of 2 kN applied to a bar of steel will cause *its size and shape to change*.
2. The shaft has *a uniform c.s.a.*
3. Copper is *a material which has the property of elasticity.*
4. An *increase in length* of 0·003 mm was found in a bar subjected to a force of 1·5 kN.
5. A body which undergoes a tensile force will *lengthen.*
6. When compressive forces *go beyond* the elastic limit permanent distortion results.
7. The body will not then return to its original *dimensions.*
8. Elastic materials *regain* their original shape and size.

EXERCISE B *Contextual reference*

1. In sentence 1, 'it' refers to   (a) stress
                                            (b) a body

2. In sentence 1, 'its' refers to   (a) the force's
                                            (b) the body's

3. In sentence 8, 'one' refers to   (a) a body
                                            (b) a tensile force

4. In sentence 9, 'its' refers to   (a) the body's
                                      (b) a force's
5. In sentence 12, 'its' refers to   (a) the elastic limit's
                                      (b) an elastic material's
6. In sentence 16, 'that' refers to (a) the graph
                                      (b) the straight line
7. In sentence 19, 'it' refers to   (a) a constant
                                      (b) an elastic material
8. In sentence 21, 'it' refers to   (a) the strain
                                      (b) the stress

EXERCISE C *Relationships between statements*

Place the following expressions in the sentences indicated. Replace or re-order the words in the sentences where necessary.

in more general terms (2)   for instance (13)
for example (7)   such as (13)
whereas (7+8)   in more general terms (15)
in contrast (8)   for this reason (16)
                                   we can conclude that (21)

II USE OF LANGUAGE

EXERCISE A *Definitions*

Make a definition for each item in column (a)

EXAMPLE
An organic material is a material which is based chemically on carbon.

a	b	c
a stainless steel		can be drawn out into wires
a non-ferrous metal		contains iron
a formable metal		is based chemically on carbon
an abrasive substance	substance	can lengthen a body
a ferrous metal	metal	resists corrosion
a compressive force	steel	does not contain iron
a ductile metal	material	can shorten a body
an organic material	force	can be shaped into forms
a tensile force		can be used to wear away a softer material

EXERCISE B *If-sentences*

From each of the definitions in Exercise A, we can make an *if*-sentence. Look at this example:

definition: An organic material is a material which is based chemically on carbon.

if-sentence: If a material is organic, it is based chemically on carbon.

Sentences like this consist of two parts joined by *if*:

PART 1   PART 2

IF   a material is organic,   /   it is based chemically on carbon

Now make *if*-sentences like this for each of the definitions you have written in Exercise A.

EXERCISE C *Predictions based on the properties of materials*

When we know what the properties of a material are we can predict how it will behave under different conditions. To make predictions of this type, we use an *if*-sentence with *will* in part 2. Look at this example:

If a material is flexible, it will bend easily.

Now write similar predictions for materials which have the properties listed in column (a). Match each property in column (a) with an appropriate expression from column (b).

a	b
elasticity	will not bend easily
plasticity	will resist abrasion, deformation and indentation
toughness	will resist wear
corrosion-resistance	will regain its original dimensions after the forces which have caused deformation are removed
rigidity	will tend to fracture under impact loads
wear-resistance	will bend easily
brittleness	will not return to its original dimensions after the forces producing strain are removed
hardness	will not fracture when indented or scratched
flexibility	will resist fracture when subjected to an impact load
softness	will resist corrosion

EXERCISE D *Noun modification* (iv)

Here is another common way of modifying a noun in engineering.

        (a) a bracket with a pin joint
=   (b) a *pin-jointed* bracket

Rewrite each of the following expressions as in example (b):
 a metal tube with thin walls
 a roller with a flat bottom
 a polygon with six sides
 a cutting tool with multiple edges
 a follower with a knife edge
 a rivet with a copper face

Describe each of the following objects as in example (a):
 a four-sided indentor
 a stellite-tipped cutting tool
 a wire-jacketed hose
 a square-threaded screw
 a round-headed rivet
 a stub-nosed tool

EXERCISE E *Prepositions*

Rewrite the following sentences, filling in the spaces with a preposition from the list. You will have to use some of the prepositions more than once.

away	of
between	on
from	to
in	with
into	

1. The crank gear meshes . . . a second gear to which the winding drum is rigidly fixed.
2. Two masses are suspended . . . the metre stick at points X and Y.
3. A single point tool consists . . . a tip made of high-speed steel and a plain carbon steel shank welded to the tip.
4. The screw runs in a fixed nut incorporated . . . the jack.
5. The worm is prevented . . . axial movements by its bearings.
6. Whether the load extends or compresses the spring depends . . . the type of balance.
7. The calculations necessary in designing gear wheels are based . . . the pitch circle diameter.
8. Vector *a–b* was converted . . . a force of 60 N.
9. Fluid is applied to cutting tools to cool and lubricate them and to wash . . . chips and swarf.
10. Brake linings are often made . . . an asbestos compound.
11. We can distinguish . . . high pressure laminates and low pressure laminates.
12. Vernier calipers are provided . . . a vernier scale to ensure accuracy in measurement.

13. A hammer with one end ball-shaped and the other end slightly domed, is referred . . . as a ball-pein hammer.
14. A single vector quantity can be resolved . . . any number of components in an infinite variety of ways.

EXERCISE F *Making inductions*

We have seen (Unit 4) that in mechanical engineering it is necessary to make inductions from observations. These observations are often written in the form of *if-* or *when-* sentences.

EXAMPLE

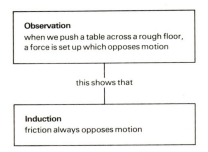

Observation
when we push a table across a rough floor,
a force is set up which opposes motion

this shows that

Induction
friction always opposes motion

Write down sentences 2, 7, 8, 11, 15, and 20 from the reading passage in your notebook. Using these sentences to help you, complete in your notebook the inductions which follow each of the observations below.

1. If a bar of iron is subjected to a force of 2 kN, it bends.
   This shows that . . . .
2. When a rod of mild steel has a compressive force of 5 kN applied to it, it contracts by 0·889 mm.
   This demonstrates that . . . .
3. If a weight of 6 kg is attached to a wire of uniform c.s.a., the wire extends by 0·05 mm.
   This shows that . . . .
4. When a load of 30 kN is applied to a steel bar, it lengthens by 0·250 mm. If the load is increased to 60 kN, the bar lengthens by 0·50 mm.
   These findings show that . . . .
5. When the load of 60 kN is removed from the steel bar, it regains its original proportions.
   This demonstrates that . . . .
6. If the load exceeds 60 kN, the bar does not return to its original size and shape when the load is removed.
   This shows that . . . .

III INFORMATION TRANSFER

EXERCISE A *Inductions based on diagrams and tables*

In the Use of Language section we learned how to make inductions from observations. In engineering we also have to make inductions from information contained in diagrams and tables. With the help of sentences 2, 7, 8, 11, 15, and 20 which you have written in your notebook, make inductions from the following diagrams and tables.

1.

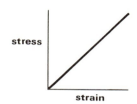

This graph shows that . . . .

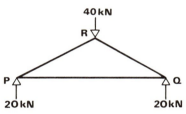

2. length of member PR off load = 330 cm
   length of member PR under load = 329·6 cm
   These figures demonstrate that . . . .
3. length of member PQ off load = 600 cm
   length of member PQ under load = 601 cm
   These figures demonstrate that . . . .

4.

applied force (-stress) kN	extension (-strain) mm
3	0·02
6	0·04
9	0·06

These figures show that . . . .

5.

tensile test results for mild steel	
stress N/mm²	extension mm
1,000	0·00066
2,000	0·00133
4,000	0·00265
6,000	0·00400
12,000	0·00795
12,100	0·09000

These results demonstrate that . . . .

EXERCISE B *Stating laws*

Inductions which are based on many observations are called *laws*. In Unit 4 some of the inductions you made were the laws of friction. These laws are written in column (b) opposite. Tables A and B contain results from a number of simple experiments on friction using the apparatus illustrated. Using the information contained in these results, write down and complete the observations in column (a). Make sure that each observation you write matches the law of friction opposite it.

apparatus

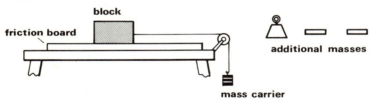

results

TABLE A

result number	nature of surfaces in contact	area of surfaces in contact	sliding friction force
		mm	N
1	wood on wood	200	10·4
2	wood on wood	100	10·4
3	wood on glass	100	6·3

TABLE B

result number	reaction between the surfaces	force required to cause movement	force required to maintain movement
	N	N	N
4	9·81	3·2	2·8
5	19·62	6·4	5·6
6	29·43	9·6	8·4

a

observations
1. Results 4, 5 and 6 show that when one surface slides over another surface, there is a force which must be overcome before. movement can occur.
2. Results 4, 5 and 6 show that if we compare . . . with the force required to maintain . . . we find that the former is . . . .
3. Results . . . 3 show that the sliding friction force for wood on wood is . . . than the . . . .
4. Results 1 and 2 show that if the . . . is halved, sliding friction force . . . .
5. Results . . . show that if the reaction between two surfaces in contact is doubled, the force . . . and the force . . . are also . . . .

b

laws
Friction always opposes motion.

Static friction is greater than sliding friction.

Friction between two surfaces depends on the nature of the surfaces in contact.
Sliding friction is independent of the area of surface in contact.

Friction is directly proportional to the reaction between the surface in contact.

Now combine each observation and law.

EXAMPLE
Results 4, 5 and 6 show that when one surface slides over another surface there is a force which must be overcome before movement can occur. This demonstrates that friction always opposes motion.

IV   GUIDED WRITING

STAGE 1 *Sentence building*

Join each of the following groups of sentences to make eleven longer sentences. You are given some, but not all, of the connecting words which you will need. You may add, omit or change words where you think it is necessary, and you should provide appropriate punctuation.

1. THUS
   From O to P the specimen extends.
   This is in proportion to the force applied to the material.
   This illustrates Hooke's law.

2. The material reaches its elastic limit.
   This happens soon after point P.
   The elastic limit is marked on the graph.
   The elastic limit is marked as point E.

3. After the yield point there is a rapid extension.
   This is an extension of the specimen.
   This rapid extension occurs with each increase in load.
   This extension continues until point U is reached.

4. WHEN
   The specimen will regain its original length up to point E.
   The forces are removed.
   The forces cause tension.

5. THAT
   This is what waisting means.
   The cross-sectional area of the specimen narrows.
   This happens at some point in the specimen's length.

6. WITHOUT
   U represents the maximum load the specimen can undergo.
   Up to this load there is no change in the specimen's cross-sectional area.

7. AFTER
   The point of maximum load is reached.
   The specimen undergoes 'waisting'.

8. HOWEVER
   If the elastic limit is exceeded.
   The specimen will not regain its original length.

9. ALTHOUGH/BECAUSE OF
   The stress continues to increase.

Note the decrease in cross-sectional area.
The load falls.

10. WHEN

The specimen lengthens further.
It lengthens until point F.
The specimen finally fractures.

11. FOR

At Y the specimen increases in length.
Y is the yield point.
This is a sudden increase.
There is very little corresponding increase in force.

STAGE 2 *Paragraph building*

Now rearrange the sentences you have written into a number of logically-ordered paragraphs. Begin your first paragraph with sentences 1 and 2.

STAGE 3   *Using diagrams to illustrate the paragraphs*

The passage you have written is intended to accompany a graph. Here is an introduction to the passage followed by the graph itself:

One of the most important mechanical tests is the tensile test to destruction in which a specimen is subjected to increasing tensile forces until it fractures. A specially prepared test-piece with a simple cross-sectional area, for example 100 mm^2, is normally used in this test. For a mild steel specimen a graph of load against extension for a tensile test may have the following appearance:

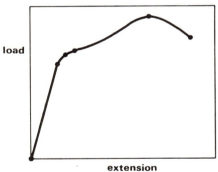

Although six points are marked on the graph they have not been labelled. Label them Y, F, O, P, U, E using the information from the paragraphs you have written.

Here are three sketches to illustrate the description. Label the sketches 'Diagram 1', 'Diagram 2' and 'Diagram 3'. Refer to your description and decide where the illustrations should be inserted into the text. Make a reference to each illustration at an appropriate place in the description, e.g.:

See Diagram 1
As shown in Diagram 1
As in Diagram 1

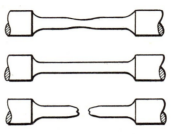

Now rewrite the entire passage, including the graph and the illustrations and any other changes you have made. Give the completed description a suitable title.

V   FREE READING

Read the following passage in your own time. If there are any words you do not know, look them up in your dictionary. Try to find additional examples of the points you have studied in this and other units.

FACTOR OF SAFETY

Designers of any stress-bearing structure, from a bracket to a suspension bridge, must accurately calculate the stresses they expect the structure to bear. They must also have a good understanding of the properties of materials. In the past, miscalculation of stresses and lack of knowledge of the properties of materials has led to disaster. For example, the first Tay Bridge in Scotland collapsed, killing 77 people, because no allowance was made for wind pressure. Even with today's testing equipment errors are sometimes made in calculating the safe loads a structure can carry. For instance, a number of box girder bridges have collapsed during construction.

To safeguard structures, designers normally work within a factor of safety so that materials are kept within their permitted working stress. Working stress is the greatest stress to which a part of a structure is ever subjected. It is calculated by dividing the ultimate strength of the material by a factor of safety. The former is the stress at which the material fractures. The latter is the product of four main factors.

The first factor is the ratio of ultimate strength to the elastic limit of the material. The elastic limit can be obtained from a tensile test. Normally this ratio is approximately 2.

The second factor depends on the nature of the stress involved. For example, a body may be exposed to one constant stress, or to variable stress, or even to compound stress, that is, where several stresses act on it at the same time. A constant stress of one kind is given a factor of 1. Variable stress is more complex. Under frequently repeated stresses a metal will fracture at a much lower point than its ultimate strength. Metal fracture caused by such stresses is commonly called 'metal fatigue'. For simply repeated stresses ranging from zero to a maximum and back to zero, a factor of 2 is allowed. For alternating stress, which not only varies in size but also in direction, for example from tensile to compressive, a factor of 3 is necessary.

The third factor concerns the application of the load. A factor of 1 may be allowed for a gradually applied load, 2 for a suddenly applied load and greater factors for shock loads.

The last factor is the most difficult to determine. Sometimes it is called the 'factor of ignorance'. If all the conditions of service are known, this factor can be low. Where the conditions of service are severe, where there is a danger of an overload or where the materials are imperfect, a factor as high as 10 may be necessary. For example, bridge builders may allow for freak winds and in earthquake zones special allowances must be made when designing tall buildings.

The following example illustrates how the factor of safety for a forged steel connecting rod in a diesel engine is calculated. The first factor is 2. As the rod is subjected alternately to both compressive and tensile stresses, the second factor is 3. When the fuel mixture ignites it imposes a suddenly applied load on the rod, hence the third factor is 2. The conditions of service of an engine are well-known, therefore the last factor is $1\frac{1}{2}$. The factor of safety is thus $2 \times 3 \times 2 \times 1\frac{1}{2}$, which equals 18.

Because of weight restrictions, aircraft are manufactured to much lower factors of safety – between 1·1 and 1·75. These extremely low factors require exacting material and production specifications and highly accurate design calculations.

In advanced design work, especially in designing skyscraper blocks, loadings up to the plastic state of metals are now used. In such design work there can be no 'factor of ignorance' and extreme accuracy in calculating the stresses on the structure is essential.

7 Ideal and Practical Machines

I READING AND COMPREHENSION

[1]A machine is any device which allows work to be done more conveniently. [2]A machine has an input member to which an effort is applied and an output member which moves a load. [3]The advantage of a machine is that the effort applied can be very much smaller than the load to be overcome. [4]The measure of this advantage is the ratio of load to effort and is known as the Mechanical Advantage (M.A.)

$$\text{M.A.} = \frac{\text{Load}}{\text{Effort}}$$

[5]In a practical machine energy is lost because of friction. [6]The M.A. of a practical machine changes as the load it carries changes because the percentage of effort required to overcome friction depends on the size of the load. [7]For very small loads a large percentage of the effort is needed to work against friction whereas with larger loads the fraction is less. [8]A graph of load against effort has the shape shown in Diagram 1:

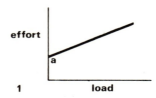

[9]In the above diagram, a is the effort required to overcome friction.

(a) The M.A. of a practical machine is a constant.
(b) A practical machine requires more effort to move small loads than large loads.
(c) A machine can lift a large load with a smaller effort.

(d) This is a graph of load against effort for a practical machine.

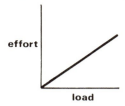

[10]To obtain a high M.A. a machine must be designed so that the distance moved by the effort is much greater than the output displacement of the load. [11]The ratio of the two distances is termed the Velocity Ratio (V.R.) that is:

$$\text{V.R.} = \frac{\text{distance moved by the effort}}{\text{distance moved by the load}}$$

[12]The V.R. of a machine depends on its design and has a fixed value for each machine. [13]In other words it is a constant.

[14]We can think of the effort which is applied to the machine as the work input. [15]The work done by the machine on the load is the work output. [16]The efficiency of the machine is then the ratio of the work output to the work input, that is:

$$\text{Efficiency} = \frac{\text{work output}}{\text{work input}}$$

[17]In practice the work output is always less than the work input because some energy is lost inside the machine in overcoming friction. [18]Thus the efficiency of a practical machine can never reach 100%. [19]Efficiency tends to increase sharply with load, then flatten out as it reaches a limiting value as shown in Diagram 2:

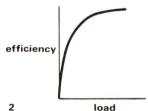

(e) The V.R. of a machine varies according to the work output.
(f) The efficiency of a practical machine is not a constant.
(g) The work input of a practical machine is greater than its work output.
(h) Efficiency is proportional to load.

[20]Mathematically it can be shown that

$$\text{Efficiency} = \frac{\text{M.A.}}{\text{V.R.}}$$

[21]An ideal machine has no friction. [22]Since an ideal machine is frictionless, its M.A. would not vary with the load but would be a constant. [23]A graph of load against effort would have the shape shown in Diagram 3:

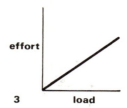

effort

3   load

[24]If it were possible to build an ideal machine, there would be no loss of energy within the machine. [25]Thus we could say that

$$\text{work input} = \text{work output}$$

i.e. $$E \times D_E = L \times D_L$$

where E = effort, D_E = distance moved by effort, L = load, and D_L = distance moved by load. [26]An ideal machine would have an efficiency of 1 or 100%. [27]As efficiency is equal to the ratio M.A./V.R. the M.A. of an ideal machine must equal its V.R.

(i) A machine with an M.A. of 5 and a V.R. of 5 is an ideal machine.
(j) For an ideal machine, efficiency would increase as the load increased.
(k) The work done by a machine on a load is equal to the load times the distance moved by the load.
(l) Frictionless machines exist.

Solutions

(a) The M.A. of a practical machine changes as the load it carries changes. (6)
=   The M.A. of a practical machine varies with the load.
∴   The M.A. of a practical machine is NOT a constant.

(b) For very small loads a large percentage of the effort is needed to work against friction whereas with larger loads the fraction is less. (7)
i.e. A practical machine requires a larger percentage of the effort to move small loads than to move large loads.
∴   It is NOT TRUE that a practical machine requires more effort to move small loads than large loads.

(c) The advantage of a machine is that the effort applied can be very much smaller than the load to be overcome. (3)
i.e. The advantage of a machine is that it can overcome a load with a very much smaller effort.
e.g. *A machine can lift a large load with a smaller effort.*

(d) A graph of load against effort has the shape shown in Diagram 1: (8).

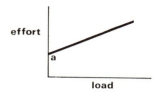

but in the graph in the question, the line passes through the origin.
i.e. There is no effort required to overcome friction.
i.e. The graph in the question is a graph of an ideal machine.
∴ The graph shown is NOT a graph of load against effort for a practical machine.

(e) The V.R. of a machine depends on its design and has a fixed value for each machine. (12) In other words it is a constant. (13)
i.e. The V.R. of a machine does not vary.
∴ It is NOT TRUE that the V.R. of a machine varies according to the work output.

(f) Efficiency tends to increase sharply with load, then flatten out as it reaches a limiting value as shown in Diagram 2. (19)
i.e. Efficiency depends on the load.
∴ *The efficiency of a practical machine is not a constant.*

(g) In practice the work output is always less than the work input because some energy is lost inside the machine. (17)
= For practical machines, the work input is greater than the work output.
i.e. *The work input of a practical machine is greater than its work output.*

(h) Efficiency tends to increase sharply with load, then flatten out as it reaches a limiting value as shown in Diagram 2: (19)

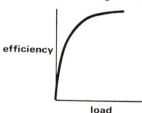

If efficiency were proportional to load, the graph would be a straight line.
∴ Efficiency is NOT proportional to load.

(i) Mathematically it can be shown that

$$\text{Efficiency} = \frac{\text{M.A.}}{\text{V.R.}} \quad (20)$$

$\therefore$ the efficiency of the machine $= \dfrac{5}{5} = 1$ or 100%

but   An ideal machine would have an efficiency of 1 or 100%. (26)

$\therefore$ *A machine with an M.A. of 5 and a V.R. of 5 is an ideal machine.*

(j)   An ideal machine would have an efficiency of 1 or 100%. (26)

i.e.   For any load the efficiency of the machine would be 100%

$\therefore$ For an ideal machine, efficiency would NOT increase as the load increased.

(k)   work input = work output

i.e. $E \times D_E = L \times D_L$

where E = effort, D_E = distance moved by effort, L = load, and D_L = distance moved by load. (25)

i.e.   Work output is equal to load times distance moved by load.

but   The work done by the machine on the load is the work output. (15)

$\therefore$ *The work done by a machine on a load is equal to the load times the distance moved by the load.*

(l)   If it were possible to build an ideal machine . . . (24)

if it were possible (here) = it is not possible

i.e.   It is not possible to build an ideal (frictionless) machine.

$\therefore$ Frictionless machines do NOT exist.

EXERCISE A *Rephrasing*

Rewrite the following, replacing the words in italics with an expression from the text which has a similar meaning.

1. The ratio of load to effort *is termed* the Mechanical Advantage.
2. Part of the effort is *needed* to overcome static and sliding friction in the machine.
3. A large *fraction* of the effort is used to *overcome* friction.
4. The *output displacement of the load* is less than the input displacement of the effort.
5. The Velocity Ratio of a machine *is a constant*.
6. *The effort which is applied to the machine* is greater than the work output.
7. *The work output of the machine* is the product of the load and the distance moved by the load.
8. An ideal machine *is frictionless*.
9. The efficiency of a practical machine *varies with the load*.

EXERCISE B *Contextual reference*

1. In sentence 2, 'which' in the phrase 'to which' refers to

    (a) a machine

    (b) an input member

    (c) an output member

2. In sentence 6, 'it' refers to   (a) the Mechanical Advantage
                                                    (b) the load
                                                    (c) a practical machine

3. In sentence 12, 'its' refers to   (a) the Velocity Ratio's
                                                    (b) a machine's
                                                    (c) a value's

4. In sentence 13, 'it' refers to   (a) the Velocity Ratio
                                                    (b) each machine
                                                    (c) a machine

5. In sentence 19, 'it' refers to   (a) a practical machine
                                                    (b) an ideal machine
                                                    (c) a load
                                                    (d) efficiency

6. In sentence 27, 'its' refers to   (a) an ideal machine's
                                                    (b) efficiency's
                                                    (c) a machine's

EXERCISE C *Relationships between statements*

Place the following expressions in the sentences indicated. Replace or re-order the words in the sentences where necessary.

since (6)   because (22)
for instance (7)   consequently (23)
on the other hand (7)   for this reason (25)
since (17)   therefore (26)
hence (18)   therefore (27)

II USE OF LANGUAGE

EXERCISE A *Predictions based on laws, generalizations and proven facts*

In Unit 6 we practised '*if*-sentences' which were predictions. These predictions were based on the properties of different materials and the sentences contained *will* in column (b). We can also make predictions based on laws, generalizations and proven facts.

EXAMPLE (based on the law 'Friction always opposes motion')
    We push a table across a rough floor.
    The motion will be opposed by friction.
    = If we push a table across a rough floor, the motion will be opposed by friction.

Now write in your notebook predictions based on the sentences in column (a). The sketches will help you to complete column (b) of each prediction.

a	b
1. We subject a steel bar to tensile forces.	The bar . . . .
2. We place a roller on a smooth inclined plane.	The roller . . . .
3. We apply an effort at E.	The block . . . .
4. We subject a strut to compressive forces.	The strut . . . .
5. We move the effort by 1 metre.	The load . . . .
6. We attach a load to a spring balance.	The spring . . . .
7. We move the effort by 50 centimetres.	The load . . . .
8. We move the effort by 1·80 metres.	The load . . . .

Now use the facts given in the table to write predictions based on the following suppositions:

COEFFICIENT OF FRICTION

surfaces	μ
bronze on bronze dry	0·20
bronze on bronze lubricated	0·05
steel on brass dry	0·35
steel on cast iron dry	0·40
leather on cast iron	0·55
plastic on cast iron	0·18
rubber on asphalt	0·65
rubber on concrete	0·70

9. We lubricate two bronze moving surfaces in contact.

Friction . . . .

10. We replace the brass bushes in which a steel shaft is running with cast iron bushes.

Friction between shaft and bushes . . . .

11. We compare braking distances for a car on asphalt roads and on concrete roads.

We will find . . . .

12. We replace a leather belt driving a cast iron pulley with a plastic belt.

The plastic belt will . . . . . under heavy loads.

EXERCISE B *Predictions based on unlikely suppositions*

Another kind of *if*-sentence is used to make predictions where the supposition is unlikely to happen.

EXAMPLE
we build an ideal machine
it will have no energy loss due to friction
= *If we built* an ideal machine, *it would have* no energy loss due to friction.

Now make predictions based on the following suppositions. First you will have to match each supposition to the appropriate sentence in column (b). Remember to change the verb in the supposition to the past tense form, and *will* in column (b) to *would*.

a	b
1. We compare work output to work input for an ideal machine.	It will be a constant.
2. We make a perfectly smooth surface.	It will be a straight line passing through the origin.
3. We measure the efficiency of an ideal machine.	We will find they are equal.
4. We draw a graph of load against effort for an ideal machine.	It will be frictionless.
5. We prepare two perfectly smooth surfaces.	We will find it is 100%.
6. We calculate the M.A. of an ideal machine.	We will find they are equal.
7. We compare the M.A. and the V.R. of an ideal machine.	It will require an effort of 20 N to raise a load of 200 N.
8. It requires an effort of 10 N to raise a load of 100 N with an ideal machine.	They will have a zero coefficient of friction with each other.

EXERCISE C *toughen, harden, soften, etc.*

Rewrite the following sentences using the verbs from the list.

roughen	lengthen	sharpen
harden	loosen	strengthen
soften	ensure	shorten
enlarge	weaken	lessen
tighten	lighten	widen

EXAMPLE

   Drills can be made sharp with grinding stone.
= Drills can be *sharpened* with grinding stone.

1. The 5 kg mass was removed to make the load on the test piece lighter.
2. A reamer can be used to make drill holes larger.
3. Repeatedly flexing copper wire makes it hard and thus makes it easy to break.
4. A torque wrench should be used to make the bolts tight on a cylinder head.
5. A tensile force will make a body longer.
6. Wing nuts can be made loose easily by hand.
7. A compressive force will tend to make a body shorter.
8. The surface should first be made rough using a coarse file.
9. Solvents can be used to make coatings soft.
10. The gap between tailstock and spindle nose can be made wider by rotating the hand wheel.

11. Friction between two rough planks can be made less if they are planed.
12. Piston rings make sure that the piston makes a gas-tight seal with the cylinder wall.
13. Extra struts will make the framework stronger.
14. Dirty materials may make reinforced concrete weak.

III INFORMATION TRANSFER

EXERCISE A *Design specifications: is to, have to, must.*

When we write about design specifications we often use *is to.*

EXAMPLES
The pulley wheel *is to* have a diameter of 120 mm.
The pulley-wheel *is to* be mounted on a power transmission shaft.

When we want to stress the importance of a design specification we use *have to* or *must.*

EXAMPLES
The width of the shoulder on the transmission shaft *has to* be not less than 9·7 mm.
The width of the shoulder *must* not exceed 10·3 mm.

Study these design specifications for a pulley wheel and the method of mounting it to a power transmission shaft:

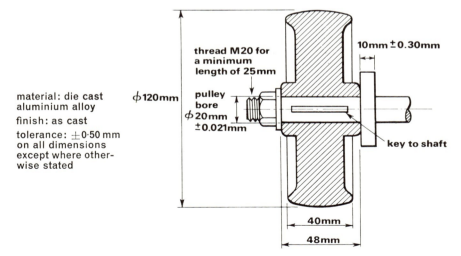

Now write down and complete the following sentences using the information contained in the diagram:

1. The pulley wheel . . . die cast aluminium alloy.
2. The pulley wheel . . . wide.
3. The end of the shaft . . . M20 . . . of 25 mm.
4. The distance through the boss of the wheel . . . greater . . . mm.
5. The diameter of the bore . . . exceed . . . mm.

EXERCISE B *Design specifications* (*continued*)

Study these design specifications for a compression spring:

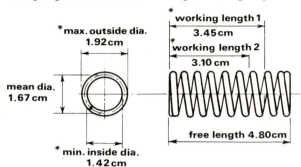

Specification				
Material	spring steel		Type of ends	closed and ground
Wire size	0·250		Wound L.H. or R.H.	L.H.
*Load to be supported at			Treatment	stress relieve
working length 1	14 kg	±1 kg	Finish	cadmium plate
*Load to be supported at				0·0005 cm/min.
working length 2	42 kg	±2·4 kg		
Total number of coils	11			
Number of free coils	9			
*Max. solid length	2·600 cm			

Note. The spring diameters may be varied within the limits stated. The number of coils may be altered if necessary providing the conditions starred thus * are maintained.

Now write nine sentences about the spring using *is to* or *have to/must* where appropriate.

EXAMPLE
    At working length 2 the spring has to support a load of 42 kg.

IV GUIDED WRITING

STAGE 1 *Sentence and paragraph building*

Join the following groups of sentences to make eleven longer sentences describing a screw-jack. You may add or omit words where you think it is necessary, and you should provide appropriate punctuation and paragraph divisions.

1. The wheel and axle, the lever, and the inclined plane are simple machines. Man has used simple machines for over 2,000 years.

2. Most machines are based on simple machines.
   The screw-jack is based on the inclined plane.
3. Cut a triangle out of paper.
   The triangle is right-angled.
   The purpose of the triangle is to represent an inclined plane.
4. Wrap the paper triangle round a cylinder.
   The inclined edge of the paper makes a spiralling line round the cylinder.
5. The spiralling line becomes the thread of the screw.
   The spiralling line is known as a helix.
6. A screw forms the main component of the screw-jack.
   The screw has a square thread.
7. Square threads are used for power transmission.
   Square threads offers less frictional resistance than vee-threads.
8. The screw is free to rotate.
   The screw rotates in a fixed nut.
   The fixed nut forms part of the body of the jack.
9. The screw rotates.
   This raises the load.
   An effort is applied to the effort bar.
10. The screw makes a full revolution.
    The load is raised by a distance.
    The load is lowered by a distance.
    The distance is equal to the pitch of the screw.
11. The pitch is a distance.
    The distance is between the same points.
    The points are on adjacent threads.

STAGE 2 *Using diagrams to illustrate the paragraphs*

Study these two drawings, then make a third drawing to show how a helix is formed from a triangle and a cylinder:

Use the following drawing to show what the pitch of a screw is:

Refer to your description, and decide where the illustrations should be inserted. Make a reference to each of the four illustrations at an appropriate place in the description. Rewrite the description and include the illustrations and any other changes you have made.

V   FREE READING

Read the following passages in your own time. If there are any words you do not know, look them up in your dictionary. Try to find additional examples of the points you have studied in this and other units.

CRANES

We can define a crane as a machine which lifts heavy loads and displaces them horizontally. In other words, a crane can lift loads and move them to a different position in the horizontal plane, unlike a hoist which is only a lifting device. We can divide cranes into two main classes. These are jib cranes and overhead travelling cranes. Jib cranes have a jib, or arm, from which the load is suspended. The jib allows the load to be raised or lowered and then deposited at any point within the radius of the jib. Movement of the jib in the vertical plane is known as derricking. The rotation of the jib in the horizontal plane is called slewing.

The commonest kind of non-revolving crane is the overhead travelling crane. Such a crane is illustrated in the diagram below. It consists of a

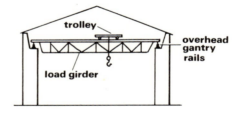

horizontal section called a load girder, made up of a number of steel beams, resting on end carriages which run on overhead gantry rails. A trolley to carry the crane hook in turn runs on top of the load girder. Cranes like this are found in workshops where heavy machinery has to be transported from place to place on the shop floor for different stages in its manufacture.

The three movements of the overhead travelling crane are as follows. It can lift a load to the height of the load girder, it can traverse the width of the shop floor with it, and it can move the load along the length of the workshop. As the body of the crane is mounted overhead it does not affect work on the shop floor as it moves. Cranes with a span of 40 metres and a maximum lifting capacity of 400 tonnes are made. For use outside a factory, for example in timber yards, a similar crane, termed a goliath crane, is used. The load girder of a goliath crane is supported not on gantry rails but on legs running on rails mounted on the ground.

There are many varieties of cranes for special purposes. They may be fixed, portable or mobile. A portable crane must be transported, whereas a mobile crane is either self-propelled or mounted on a truck chassis or a railway wagon. Cranes use different forms of power, for example electric power, diesel power, hydraulic power, steam power and even hand power are used depending on the type of crane and its application.

An example of a crane with a particular application is the shipyard crane. This is a heavy, fixed crane with a slewing cantilever mounted on a latticed tower which is firmly anchored in concrete. In addition to the main load trolley the crane may be fitted with a small jib crane running on the cantilever. Such cranes are necessary in shipbuilding because when a ship is being fitted out, heavy machinery, such as the engines, has to be lowered into the vessel. These cranes must be capable of placing the loads inside the ship with great accuracy. For this reason some form of fine electrical control is normally employed.

Another example is the dockside crane which is used to unload and load ships. It is usually mounted on rails which run the length of the quay and is often fitted with a grab instead of a hook. A grab has two jaws which open and close like a clamshell. It is designed to handle bulk cargoes like iron ore and gravel. One variety of dockside crane, known as a kangaroo crane, feeds bulk cargoes directly into a hopper at its base. From the hopper the cargo is weighed and discharged into trucks and railway wagons.

8 The Four-Stroke Petrol Engine

I READING

PART 1 *The carburettor*

Complete the labelling of the diagram using the words in italics in the passage. Write down the labels in your notebook against the letters a–j.

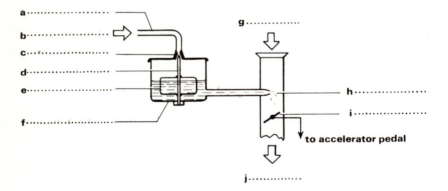

[1]The carburettor is a device which provides the engine with an air and petrol mixture in the correct proportions for all running conditions. [2]This simplified diagram shows how it operates. [3]*Petrol* enters the *float chamber* via the *feed pipe* and the *fuel inlet*. [4]When the chamber is filled to the correct level, the *float* and *needle-valve* rise, cutting off the fuel supply. [5]When the piston moves down the cylinder it reduces the pressure within the cylinder. [6]The pressure of the atmosphere then pushes *air* in through the carburettor where it mixes with a fine *jet of petrol* from the float chamber to produce finely divided fuel droplets. [7]The quantity of this *atomized fuel* which enters the cylinder is controlled by a *throttle valve*. [8]In a motor car the throttle valve is opened and closed by operating the accelerator pedal.

PART 2 *The valves*

Complete the passage using the information in the diagram. Write down a list of the missing words against their sentence numbers.

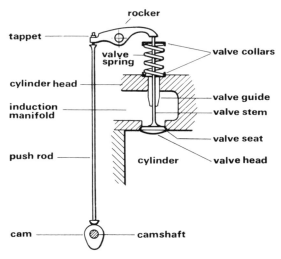

[9]The function of the valves is to open and close at the correct time when the engine is running so that fuel can enter the cylinder and the exhaust gases escape. [10]The valve illustrated is an inlet valve. [11]It is fitted into the . . . . [12]Fuel from the . . . enters the . . . through it. [13]The . . . is ground so that it fits the . . . exactly, forming a gas-tight seal. [14]The . . . slides through a . . . , which is a sleeve of bronze tapered at one end so that it can be driven tightly into the cylinder-head.

[15]The inlet valve is kept closed by means of a . . . . [16]The ends of the spring are held between two . . . . [17]One collar is set in the cylinder head while the upper collar is attached to the valve stem.

[18]The valve is opened at the right moment by means of a . . . mounted on a . . . . [19]This shaft is driven by the engine crankshaft. [20]As the cam turns it pushes up the . . . which in turn raises one end of the . . . . [21]The other end presses down on the valve stem and the valve opens. [22]A small screw, called the . . . , is provided at one end of the rocker to allow slight adjustments to be made in the proportion of the lift from the cam being imparted to the valve.

PART 3 *The four-stroke cycle*

Read the following passage carefully and write down a list of the missing words against their sentence numbers. Use the diagrams on page 94 to help you. These diagrams represent the four strokes in the cycle. They are not in the correct order and they are not named. Write down the names of each of the strokes represented.

[23]In the four-stroke petrol engine there is a sequence, or cycle of events which is completed in four strokes of the piston. [24]The events which take place in each stroke are as follows:

induction stroke   [25]With the . . . open and the exhaust valve shut, the piston moves down the cylinder creating a partial vacuum. [26]This partial vacuum draws in the atomized fuel from the . . . into the cylinder.

compression stroke   [27]With both the inlet and exhaust valves closed, the . . . moves up the cylinder, compressing the fuel mixture. [28]Just before the end of the stroke, an electric spark across the points of the . . . ignites the petrol and air mixture.

power stroke   [29]Both valves remain closed. [30]During the tiny interval of time required for the flame to establish itself, the piston has reached its highest position in the . . . . [31]The gas generated by the burning fuel now expands rapidly, driving the piston down the cylinder. [32]This downward push is converted into a rotary movement by the connecting rod and . . . . [33]A . . . contained within the cylinder wall helps to conduct away the heat generated during this burning and thus keeps the engine cool.

exhaust stroke   [34]The exhaust valve opens but the inlet valve remains shut. [35]The piston moves up the cylinder, pushing the exhaust gas out through the . . . . [36]With the completion of the exhaust stroke the cycle begins again.

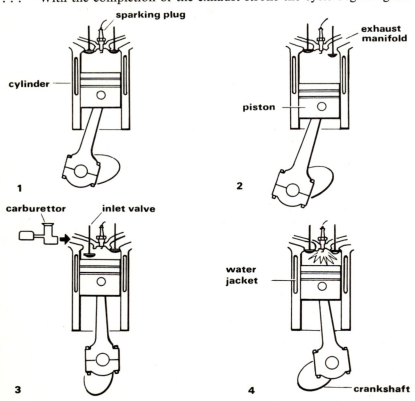

II USE OF LANGUAGE

EXERCISE A *Cause and effect*

We can sometimes use an *-ing* clause to link a 'cause' and an 'effect'.

EXAMPLES

    cause: The piston travels up the cylinder.
    effect: The piston compresses the mixture.
           The piston travels up the cylinder, compressing the mixture.

    cause: The gas expands suddenly.
    effect: This drives the piston down the cylinder.
           The gas expands suddenly, driving the piston down the cylinder.

Now join the following cause and effect pairs in the same way:

cause	*effect*
1. The piston moves down the cylinder.	This creates a partial vacuum.
2. The inlet valve opens.	This allows the fuel mixture to enter the cylinder.
3. The rocker tilts to the right.	It pushes the valve down.
4. A poppet valve drops after two milliseconds.	The valve shuts off the fuel supply.
5. The worm-gear revolves once.	This turns the wheel a distance equal to the lead of the worm.
6. A tensile force is applied to the bar.	It stretches the bar by 0·09 mm.
7. The screw revolves once.	It raises the load by 30 mm.
8. The drum unwinds 100 metres in 20 seconds.	It lowers the pit-cage at a velocity of 5 m/s.
9. The brakes are applied when the car has a speed of 54 km/h.	They reduce its speed to 20 km/h.
10. As the governor spins, the weights pull outwards.	This raises the shaft collar and reduces the fuel supply to the engine.

EXERCISE B *Problems and solutions*

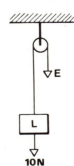

Look at this example:

problem   *solution*
Raise the load.   Apply a force at E greater than 10 N.

We can join the 'problem' and the 'solution' in various ways:

(a) To raise the load, apply a force at E greater than 10 N.
(b) We raise the load by applying a force at E greater than 10 N.
(c) The load is raised by applying a force at E greater than 10 N.

Now write down a solution for each of the following problems. Then combine problem and solution in a sentence, using pattern (a), (b) or (c).

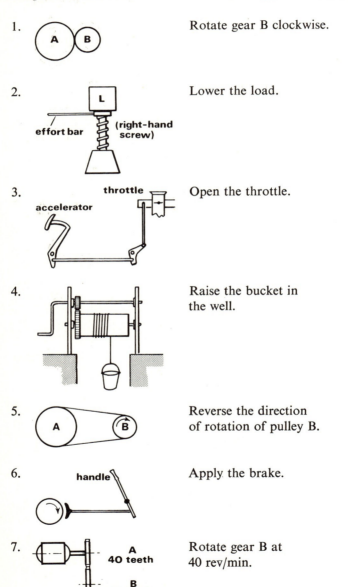

1.   Rotate gear B clockwise.

2.   Lower the load.

3.   Open the throttle.

4.   Raise the bucket in the well.

5.   Reverse the direction of rotation of pulley B.

6.   Apply the brake.

7.   Rotate gear B at 40 rev/min.

8.    Rotate gear B clockwise.

9.   Raise load L.

10.   Rotate gear B at
    50 rev/min anti-clockwise.

100 teeth   50 teeth

EXERCISE C *-tight, -proof, -resistant*

The ending *-tight* is used to describe joints, and the endings *-proof* and *-resistant* describe materials which have certain properties.

EXAMPLES

an air-tight connection
= a connection *which* air *cannot pass through*

a heat-resistant material
= a material *which is not damaged by* heat

-proof has two meanings:

a moisture-proof coating
= a coating *which* moisture *cannot pass through*

an acid-proof cement
= a cement *which is not damaged by* acid

Now describe the following materials and joints:

a gas-tight seal
an oil-proof cement
a water-resistant grease
a light-proof coating
a water-tight connection

a sound-proof engine cladding
a rust-proof surface
a shock-proof mounting
a corrosion-resistant steel
a weather-proof surface

III   INFORMATION TRANSFER

EXERCISE A *Describing the shapes of objects*

SHAPE	NOUN	ADJECTIVE	SHAPE	NOUN	ADJECTIVE
2 dimensional			3 dimensional		
◯	circle	circular	(sphere)	sphere	spherical
⌒	semi-circle	semi-circular	(cube)	cube	cubical
▢	square	square	(rectangular block)		rectangular
▭	rectangle	rectangular	(cylinder)	cylinder	cylindrical
△	triangle	triangular	(cone)	cone	conical
⬭	ellipse	elliptical	**lines**		straight
					curved
⬡	hexagon	hexagonal	**edges** a. b.		a. round
					b. pointed

When an object has a regular geometric shape we can use one of the adjectives from the table above to describe it.

EXAMPLE

a square faceplate

When the object has no recognized geometric shape but does resemble a well-known object or a letter of the alphabet, it may be described in one of the following ways:

EXAMPLES

a mushroom-shaped valve
a valve shaped like a mushroom

a V-shaped cut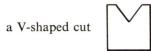

Now describe the shapes of the following objects as completely as possible.

1. piston

2. slot for a turbine blade

3. rivet head

4. side plate

5. caliper gauge

6. nut

7. Wankel engine piston

8. pulley belt – cross-section

9. furnace combustion chamber

10. spray from a fuel injection nozzle

11. groove in the block

12. face plate

13. the point of the lathe centre

14. cross-section of a wooden beam

15. cross-section of a steel beam

16. cross-section of a steel beam

IV GUIDED WRITING

STAGE 1 *Sentence and paragraph building*

Write a description of pistons based on the following notes. Combine the sentences in any way you wish, adding or omitting material where you think it is necessary. You should divide your description into several paragraphs.

Pistons are cylindrical.
Pistons are cup-shaped.
Pistons are cast from steel or aluminium alloy.
Aluminium conducts heat well.
This helps the pistons to cool quickly.
The upper end of the piston is called the crown.
The upper end is closed.
The walls of the piston are known as the skirt.
These are machined to fit the cylinder closely.
The crown forms the lower part of the combustion chamber.
It is normally flat.
It can be domed.
It can be dished.
The piston walls are grooved.
There are several grooves near the top.
There is one groove near the bottom.
The grooves are for piston rings.
Piston rings are circles of grey cast iron.
The rings have a small gap in them.
The rings have a larger diameter than the cylinder when they are unstressed.
When they are stressed they make a tight fit with the cylinder walls.
The rings have two functions.

The top rings keep gas from escaping from the combustion chamber.
The bottom ring is called the oil-control ring.
The bottom ring keeps the flow of oil to the minimum necessary.
The oil lubricates the rings and the pistons.
The bottom ring clears surplus oil from the cylinder walls.
A hole through the piston holds the gudgeon pin.
The gudgeon pin connects the piston and the connecting rod.
The gudgeon pin should be of the floating type.
The gudgeon pin should be hollow.
The piston must be well designed.
The piston is subjected to compressive stress.
The piston must withstand repeated impact loads.
The piston must withstand heat.
The piston must move up and down at an average speed of 13 m/s in automobile engines.

STAGE 2 *Using diagrams to illustrate the passage*

Copy the following diagram into your notebook, label it and use it to illustrate your description.

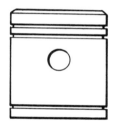

V FREE READING

Read the following passage in your own time. If there are any words you don't know, look them up in your dictionary. Try to find additional examples of the points you have studied in this and other units.

THE WANKEL ENGINE

The Wankel engine is a form of heat engine which has a rotary piston. In other words, instead of going up and down the Wankel piston rotates in the cylinder. Both cylinder and piston are quite different in shape from those of conventional engines. The Wankel piston is triangular with curved sides and the cylinder is roughly oval in shape. The piston has an inner bore which is linked through an eccentric gear to the output shaft. The other end of the bore is toothed and engages with a stationary gear fixed to the cylinder end. This arrangement ensures that the piston follows an elliptical path round the cylinder so that the apexes of the piston, which carry gas-tight seals, are always in contact with the inside surface of the cylinder.

The piston thus forms three crescent-shaped spaces between itself and the cylinder wall, which vary in size as the piston rotates. Fuel enters the cylinder through the inlet port when one of these spaces is increasing in size. The fuel trapped in this section is then compressed by the turning piston and ignited by the sparking plug. The expanding gases subject the

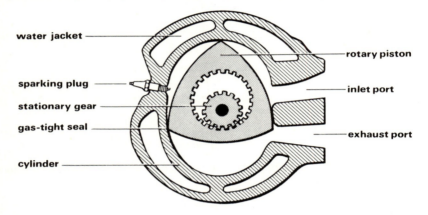

piston to a twisting moment which makes the piston revolve further until the exhaust gases escape through the exhaust port. A fresh charge is then induced into the cylinder. Meanwhile the same process is being repeated in the other two spaces between the piston and the cylinder.

The Wankel engine has many advantages over the reciprocating piston engine. Fewer moving parts are necessary because it produces a rotary movement without using a connecting rod and a crankshaft. Because of this rotary movement it has no vibration. In addition it has no valves, it is smaller and lighter than conventional engines of the same power, and it runs economically on diesel and several other fuels.

QUESTIONS ON FREE READING PASSAGES

UNIT 1 *Corrosion*

1. What is corrosion?
2. How does corrosion make a structure more expensive?
3. How do stainless steels resist corrosion?
4. Why is Monel metal used for marine engine parts?
5. What are cupronickels and what special properties do they have?
6. What is electrolytic corrosion caused by?
7. How can corrosion be controlled?

UNIT 2 *Scales and Graphs*

1. What is a vector used for?
2. How can we describe a scalar quantity?
3. In what way is a thermometer a scale?
4. Name two uses of scales.
5. What is a slide-rule and what is it used for?
6. Name two ways in which a relationship between two variables can be shown.
7. Describe the advantages of a graph.
8. Give one difference between a graph and a nomograph.

UNIT 3 *Gravity*

1. What kind of force is gravity?
2. What is weight?
3. When does weightlessness occur?
4. Why won't normal pens write in weightless conditions?
5. Why do people weigh less on the moon?
6. What error do we make in assuming that gravity always exerts a force of 9·81 N on a body for every kilogramme of its mass?

UNIT 4 *Lubrication*

1. Explain how a screw-jack depends on friction.
2. Why is it important that friction is high between a belt and a pulley wheel?
3. What are the disadvantages of friction?
4. Why do two polished steel surfaces weld together only at a few points?
5. Why is static friction between steel surfaces greater than sliding friction?
6. How does oil reduce friction?
7. Why cannot power loss be eliminated by lubrication?
8. What factors influence the choice of a lubricant?

UNIT 5 *Beams*

1. What effect does a load have on a horizontal beam?
2. What kind of stress stretches a material?
3. If the beam shown in Diagram 1 were two metres longer, what effect would this have on the bending moments?
4. Why is it not necessary to have a lot of steel in the web of a beam?
5. How is a castellated girder made?
6. What advantage does a castellated girder have over a normal beam?
7. Why is the depth of a beam important?

UNIT 6 *Factor of safety*

1. What is working stress?
2. How is the elastic limit of a material calculated?
3. In calculating the second factor, what kind of stress requires the smallest factor of safety?
4. What causes metal fatigue?
5. Describe alternating stress and give an example of a common piece of machinery which is subjected to it.
6. When estimating the 'factor of ignorance' what must the engineer consider?
7. Why does the third factor have a value of 2 for the connecting rod?
8. Why are aircraft manufactured to low factors of safety?

UNIT 7 *Cranes*

1. What is the difference between a hoist and a crane?
2. What are jib cranes?
3. What are the two horizontal movements of an overhead travelling crane?
4. What is a goliath crane?
5. Why do shipyard cranes require fine electrical control for raising and lowering the crane hook?
6. Describe the operation of a kangaroo crane.
7. When is a grab used instead of a hook?
8. Explain the difference between a mobile and a portable crane.

UNIT 8 *The Wankel engine*

1. How is the output shaft connected to the piston?
2. How are the combustion chambers formed?
3. What happens in a Wankel engine when the fuel mixture is ignited?
4. Why does a Wankel engine not vibrate?
5. Write a comparison of the Wankel engine and the conventional internal-combustion engine in not more than 100 words.

Key to the Exercises

UNIT 1
I

A 1. an alloy (6), 2. may be added to (9)+(8), 3. types (12), 4. employed (14), 5. withstand (14).

B 1. (b), 2. (a), 3. (b), 4. (a), 5. (b).

II
A

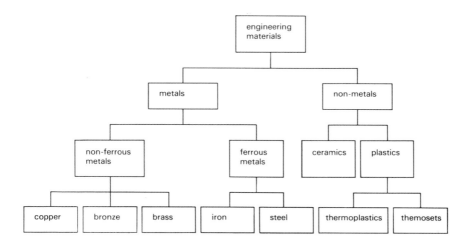

B *Diagrams*

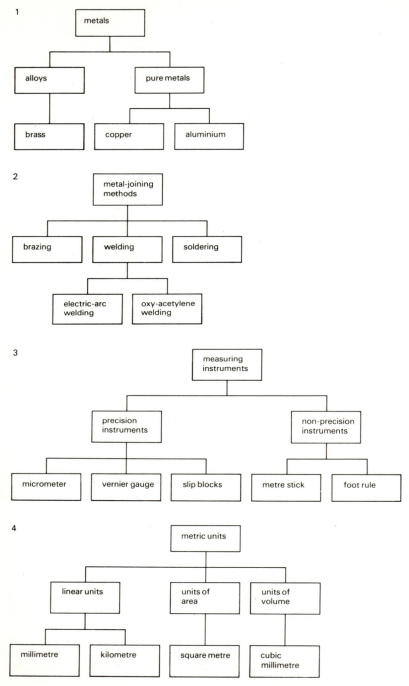

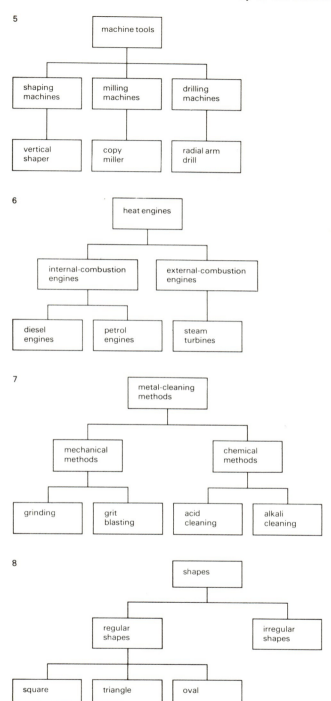

5

machine tools

- shaping machines
  - vertical shaper
- milling machines
  - copy miller
- drilling machines
  - radial arm drill

6

heat engines

- internal-combustion engines
  - diesel engines
  - petrol engines
- external-combustion engines
  - steam turbines

7

metal-cleaning methods

- mechanical methods
  - grinding
  - grit blasting
- chemical methods
  - acid cleaning
  - alkali cleaning

8

shapes

- regular shapes
  - square
  - triangle
  - oval
- irregular shapes

Note: No example of an irregular shape is given

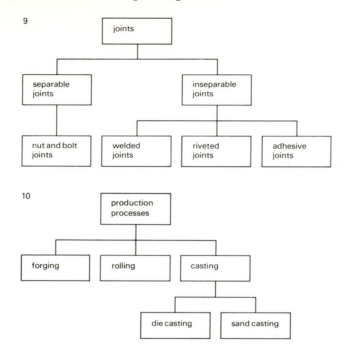

9

```
                    ┌─────────────┐
                    │   joints    │
                    └─────────────┘
              ┌───────────┴───────────┐
    ┌─────────────┐           ┌─────────────┐
    │ separable   │           │ inseparable │
    │ joints      │           │ joints      │
    └─────────────┘           └─────────────┘
          │          ┌──────────┼──────────┐
  ┌─────────────┐ ┌─────────┐ ┌────────┐ ┌──────────┐
  │ nut and bolt│ │ welded  │ │ riveted│ │ adhesive │
  │ joints      │ │ joints  │ │ joints │ │ joints   │
  └─────────────┘ └─────────┘ └────────┘ └──────────┘
```

10

```
              ┌──────────────┐
              │ production   │
              │ processes    │
              └──────────────┘
        ┌────────────┼────────────┐
   ┌─────────┐ ┌─────────┐ ┌─────────┐
   │ forging │ │ rolling │ │ casting │
   └─────────┘ └─────────┘ └─────────┘
                      ┌──────────┴──────────┐
              ┌──────────────┐   ┌──────────────┐
              │ die casting  │   │ sand casting │
              └──────────────┘   └──────────────┘
```

①B *Sentences*

2. Metal-joining methods can be classified as brazing, welding and soldering. Electric-arc and oxy-acetylene welding are examples of welding.

3. Measuring instruments can be classified as precision and non-precision instruments. Slip blocks are an example of precision instruments and the foot rule is an example of a non-precision instrument.

4. Metric units can be classified as linear units, units of area and units of volume. The kilometre is an example of a linear unit, the square metre is an example of a unit of area and the cubic metre is an example of a unit of volume.

5. Machine tools may be classified as shaping machines, milling machines and drilling machines. The vertical shaper is an example of a shaping machine. The copy miller is an example of a milling machine and the radial arm drill is an example of a drilling machine.

6. Heat engines can be classified as internal-combustion engines and external-combustion engines. Diesel engines and petrol engines are examples of internal-combustion engines and steam turbines are examples of external-combustion engines.

7. Metal-cleaning methods can be classified as mechanical and non-mechanical methods. Grinding is an example of a mechanical method and alkali cleaning is an example of a chemical method.

8. Shapes can be classified as regular and irregular shapes. The square is an example of a regular shape.

9. Joints can be classified as separable and inseparable joints. Nut and bolt joints are examples of separable joints and welded and riveted joints are examples of inseparable joints.

10. Production procésses may be classified as forging, rolling and casting. Die-casting and sand-casting are examples of casting.

①C 1. Chromium resists corrosion, therefore it is added to steels to make them rust proof.
2. Cutting tools are made from high-speed steels because these steels retain their cutting edge at high temperatures.
3. Under normal conditions aluminium resists corrosion; however serious corrosion occurs in salt water.
4. Manganese steel is very hard, therefore it is used for armour plate.
5. Bronze has a low coefficient of friction, therefore it is used to make bearings.
6. Nylon is used to make fibres and gears because it is tough and has a low coefficient of friction.
7. Tin is used to coat other metals to protect them because it resists corrosion.
8. Tin is expensive, therefore the coats of tin applied to other metals are very thin.
9. Stainless steels require little maintenance and have a high strength; however they are expensive and difficult to machine at high speeds.
10. Nickel, cobalt and chromium improve the properties of metals, therefore they are added to steels.

F

force	newton	N
time	second	s
mass	kilogramme	kg
length and distance	metre	m
area	square metre	m^2
volume	cubic metre	m^3

1. Velocity is measured in metres per second. m/s. Velocity is found by dividing a distance by a time.
2. Pressure is measured in newtons per square metre. N/m^2. Pressure is found by dividing a force by an area.
3. Density is measured in kilogrammes per cubic metre. kg/m^3. Density is found by dividing a mass by a volume.
4. Stress is measured in newtons per square millimetre. N/mm^2. Stress is found by dividing a force by an area.
5. Acceleration is measured in metres per second squared. m/s^2. Acceleration is found by dividing a distance by a time.

III

A 1. The steel rod is twelve metres long.
2. The steel plate has an area of eight square metres.
3. The weight has a mass of twenty kilogrammes.
4. The electricity pylon is twenty-five metres high.
5. The oil tank has a capacity of nine cubic metres.
The oil is six cubic metres in volume.
6. The brick is of mass three kilogrammes.
7. The beam is one hundred and twenty millimetres wide.
The flange of the beam is one hundred and twenty millimetres in width.
The beam has a depth of four hundred millimetres.
8. The block is point double zero seven five cubic metres in volume.
The length of the block is five hundred millimetres.
The block is one hundred and fifty millimetres in width.
The block is one hundred millimetres thick.
9. The pipe has a wall thickness of two point five millimetres.
10. The casting has a mass of thirty grammes.
11. The steel plate is two hundred millimetres wide.
The steel plate is ten millimetres thick.
12. The crowbar has a length of one point seven metres.

IV *Plastics*

Plastics are used widely in engineering because they are cheap and have a resistance to atmospheric corrosion; however they are not particularly strong. There are two types of plastics – thermoplastics and thermosets. Thermoplastics will soften when heated and will harden when cooled whereas thermosets will set on heating and will not remelt. Plastics are used to make a great variety of products from textiles to engineering components. Plastics are available in many forms such as sheets, tubes, rods, moulding powders and resins.

Various methods are used to convert raw plastic into finished products. Compression moulding is a common method used for shaping thermosets. The equipment consists of a press with two heated platens which carry an upper and a lower mould. Moulding powder is placed in the lower mould then the upper mould is pressed down on the lower mould. The pressure and the heat change the powder to liquid plastic which fills the space between the moulds. When the chemical changes have taken place, the mould is opened and the moulding is extracted. Plastic bowls are made by the compression moulding method.

UNIT 2

I

A 1. measure (5), 2. shows (14), 3. possess (3), 4. indicates (11), 5. magnitude (3).

B 1. (a), 2. (a), 3. (a), 4. (b), 5. (b).

C NOTE: other word orders may be acceptable.

Mass, volume and length are examples of scalar quantities. (4)
Therefore force is a vector quantity. (6)
For example, the straight line *a–b* in the diagram is a vector which represents a force. (9)
In addition the direction of the line indicates the direction of the force. (11)
Thus the line is vertical because the direction of the force it represents is vertical. (12)
For this reason the arrow-head on the line shows that the sense of direction of the force is upwards. (14)

II

A

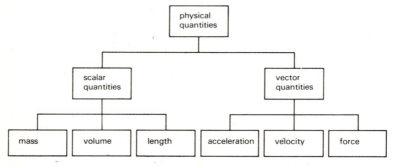

NOTE: The following is not a complete list of all the sentences which can be made from the above diagram. It illustrates however the types of sentence which can be made.

Mass is a scalar quantity. Mass, volume and length are scalar quantities.
Acceleration and velocity are vector quantities.
Volume is a physical quantity. Length and acceleration are physical quantities.

B A vector quantity is a physical quantity which has magnitude and direction.
A load is a force which can stretch or compress a body.
A tensile force is a force which can extend a body.
A linear dimension is a dimension which can be measured in a straight line.
A vector is a straight line which represents a vector quantity.
A compressive force is a force which can compress a body.
A derived unit is a unit which is a product of basic units.
Friction is a force which opposes motion.

C A vector quantity has magnitude and direction.
A load can stretch or compress a body.
A tensile force can extend a body.
A linear dimension can be measured in a straight line.
A vector represents a vector quantity.
A compressive force can compress a body.
A derived unit is a product of basic units.
Friction opposes motion.

①D 2. Bronze contains copper and tin.
3. A square metre is made by multiplying a metre by a metre.
4. Chromium makes steel corrosion-resistant.
5. A load of five tonnes compresses a concrete column.
6. Zirconia heat shields withstand temperatures over 2,000° C.
7. Vinylite can be shaped in a lathe.
8. Railway lines extend in hot weather.
9. Four-stroke internal combustion engines burn petrol, diesel oil and gas.

Alloys are mixtures of metals.
Derived units are products of basic units.
Metallic elements are added to steel to improve its properties.
Compressive forces shorten bodies.

Ceramics can resist high temperatures.
Plastics may be machined.
Metals expand when heated.
Engines consume fuel.

III
A+B 1. x–y is a vector. It represents a force of three hundred newtons. The force acts vertically upwards.
x–y is a vector which represents a force of three hundred newtons acting vertically upwards.
2. c–d is a vector. It represents a force of two kilonewtons. The force acts in an upwards direction at sixty degrees to the horizontal.
c–d is a vector which represents a force of two kilonewtons acting in an upwards direction at an angle of sixty degrees to the horizontal.
3. a–b is a vector. It represents an acceleration of twenty metres per second squared. The acceleration is in a north-westerly direction.
a–b is a vector which represents an acceleration of twenty metres per second squared in a north-westerly direction.
4. x–y is a vector. It represents a force of one hundred and eighty newtons. The force acts vertically downwards.
x–y is a vector which represents a force of one hundred and eighty newtons acting vertically downwards.
5. p–q is a vector. It represents an acceleration of thirty metres per second squared. The acceleration is in a north-easterly direction.
p–q is a vector which represents an acceleration of thirty metres per second squared in a north-easterly direction.

IV

If a smooth roller is placed on an inclined plane, it will run down the plane. A force must be applied to the roller to keep it in equilibrium. This force can be applied in any direction providing one component acts up the plane. In the diagram, this force – P – is shown acting parallel to the plane. The roller is acted on by two other forces. One is the force due to gravity – F_g – which can be considered to act vertically downwards through the midpoint of the roller. The third force is called the normal reaction – R. As the roller and plane are assumed to be absolutely smooth, this reaction is at right angles to the surface of the plane. It is now found that we have an example of a three-force system.

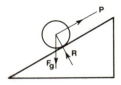

UNIT 3

I

A 1. stretch (8), 2. gravity (11), 3. matched (18), 4. by itself (14), 5. natural force (13), 6. gravity (11), 7. gun (18), 8. acts (16).

B 1. (b), 2. (b), 3. (a), 4. (a), 5. (a).

C NOTE: other word orders may be acceptable.
On the other hand a force can stop something moving or hinder motion. (5)
For example, if we brake a moving car it will slow down and eventually stop. (6)
In addition, forces may compress, bend or even break an object. (9)
Thus if we pick up a stone, then release it, it falls to the ground because of gravitational force. (12)
For example, gravity is a natural force. (13)
For this reason when a force acts on a rigid body it is balanced by an equal reaction force. (16)
A further example is that if a man fires a rifle. . . . (18)

II

A+B+C 1. If we push against a small object it moves.
2. When a moving car is braked it stops/it slows down and eventually stops.
3. If a heavy mass is suspended from a copper wire, the wire extends.
4. A heavy weight falls to the ground when it is released from a height of one metre.
5. If we stand on slippery ground and push against a heavy load our feet slide backwards.
6. When we hold a gun against our shoulder and fire it, the gun pushes backwards against our shoulder.
7. A thin metal rod bends/buckles if a force of 500 N is applied to it.
8. An iron casting breaks/fractures if we apply a force of 2 kN suddenly to it.
9. When we apply a load of 1 kN to the end of a steel upright the upright is compressed.
10. If we apply a force to a rigid body the force is balanced by an equal reaction force.
11. The spring extends when a brick is suspended from a spring balance.
12. If a piece of glass is struck with a hammer the glass breaks.

①D 1. A strut is a member which resists a compressive force.
2. The beams which form the chassis of the truck are welded together.
3. Rust may attack certain metals which contain some proportion of iron.
4. We can combine information on the size of a force and the distance it moves, in a diagram which is called a work diagram.
5. Sir Isaac Newton put forward the law which states that every action has an equal and opposite reaction.

①E 1. The rectangular block of steel, which measures 100 by 200 by 10 mm, is fixed to the floor.
2. The electric motor, which has a mass of 400 kg, is linked to the driving shaft by a belt.
3. Polished steel, which is normally described as flat and smooth, is in fact covered with tiny bumps.
4. Friction, which is always present in a machine, dissipates mechanical energy by converting it into heat energy.
5. Stainless steel contains chromium, which makes the steel corrosion-resistant.

①F 1. The body is just on the point of sliding at the angle which is known as the angle of friction. (defining)
2. A railway engine, which has a mass of 80 tonnes, draws a train of eight coaches, each of mass 17 tonnes, up a gradient of 1 in 40. (non-defining)
3. The screw-jack is basically a screw running through a fixed nut which is incorporated in the jack. (defining)
4. As the cord is wound off the wheel, the load cord, which is attached to the axle, is wound on and thus overcomes the load. (non-defining)
5. The gear which is last in an even series of gears in mesh rotates in an opposite direction to the first. (defining)
6. Intermediate gears, which do not affect the ratio of the gear train, are often referred to as idlers. (non-defining)
7. Hoisting winches of the first group, which employ a simple gear train, are termed single purchase crab winches. (non-defining)
8. This diagram means that the tensile force which will cause permanent distortion must exceed three kN. (defining)
9. Complicated mechanisms which make up an aeroplane engine are machines just as simple levers are machines. (defining)
10. Malleable cast iron, which is a ferrous metal, is tougher than grey cast iron. (non-defining)
11. Steels which are used to make tools are called tool steels. (defining)
12. The Kariba dam, which is situated on the Zambesi, provides electric power for Zambia. (non-defining)

①G air motor   (a)   electric drill   (a)
turret lathe   (d)   metal casting   (b)
chromium steel   (c)   concrete bridge   (b)
steel plate   (b)   heat engine   (a)
wing nut   (d)   aluminium alloy   (c)

Wankel engine – an engine invented by Wankel
heat treatment – treatment by heat
force system – a system of forces
hand pump – a pump operated by hand
needle valve – a valve shaped like a needle
dockside crane – a crane which is used at a dockside
test piece – a piece used in a test or a piece subjected to a test
water tube – a tube which carries water

fuel gas – a gas used as a fuel
instrument lathe – a lathe used for making instruments
gear lubricant – a lubricant used for gears
mushroom valve – a valve shaped like a mushroom

III

A 1. force is proportional to mass times acceleration.
2. power equals work done over time taken.
3. one radian is approximately equal to fifty-seven point three degrees.
4. efficiency is equal to useful output divided by input times one hundred per cent.
5. plus or minus zero point one five millimetres on all dimensions.
6. six thousand eight hundred and twenty square millimetres is equal to six thousand eight hundred and twenty times ten to the power minus six square metres.
7. air to petrol (ratio) is equal to fifteen to one.
8. g (acceleration due to gravity) is approximately equal to nine point eight one metres per second squared.
9. four hundred square millimetres area is equivalent to fifty joules.
10. power is equal to F times v.

B 1. tangent phi equals mu.
2. one radian equals one eighty degrees divided by pi (which) is approximately equal to fifty-seven point three degrees.
3. power absorbed by the brake is equal to mu R times two pi r times n watts.
4. average speed between P and Q is equal to the ratio of delta s to delta t.
5. R equals the square root of sigma P_X (all) squared, plus sigma P_Y (all) squared.
6. pitch is equal to two h times the tangent half phi.
7. efficiency equals eta (which) is equal to the ratio of MA to VR.
8. force required to hold the body at rest is equal to m_g sine theta newtons.
9. V equals one-third/one over three pi r cubed times cotangent (of) alpha.
10. theta is equal to omega times t plus half alpha times t squared.
11. b equals half p secant half beta.
12. gamma equals twenty-six degrees thirty-four minutes.

IV *Stability*

We can think of the weight of a body as acting at one point, which is known as the body's centre of gravity. A body will always act as if its mass were concentrated at its centre of gravity although its centre of gravity need not be within the body itself. The centre of gravity of some regular shapes, such as a cube, can be found by inspection. It is easy to make such regular shapes stand upright; for example, a cylinder will stand on its base. If a body is to stand upright, the line of action of its weight, which passes through its centre of gravity, must act through the base. For example, if a rectangular solid is placed on one face its weight will act through the centre of the base, and therefore the solid will stand upright as demonstrated by Diagram 1. If the solid is tilted slightly, the line of action of its weight will move towards the edge of the base but it will still fall within the base. This is illustrated by Diagram 2. If the solid is tilted further, the line drawn vertically downwards from its centre of gravity will fall outside the base, therefore the solid will topple over as shown in Diagram 3.

If a body returns to its original position after a slight disturbance it is said to be stable, whereas if a body moves into a new position after a slight disturbance it is said to be unstable. Because unstable structures can be dangerous, they have to be stabilized. For instance, cranes are normally stabilized by a large counterweight which ensures that the total mass of the crane and its load always acts through the crane's base. In addition, cranes often have a warning device which operates when the safe load is exceeded so that the crane is never in danger of toppling over.

UNIT 4

I

A 1. opposes (2), 2. reduced (4), 3. sliding friction (7), 4. in contact (18), 5. doubled (16), 6. motion (2).

B 1. (a), 2. (a), 3. (b), 4. (b), 5. (b).

C NOTE: other word orders may be acceptable.
On the other hand, the force which must be overcome to keep one surface moving over another is known as sliding friction. (7)
This slightly greater force is called static friction, whereas the force which must be overcome to keep one surface moving over another is known as sliding friction. (6+7)
In more general terms, static friction is greater than sliding friction. (8)
For instance, friction between two rough planks can be lessened if they are made smooth. (10)
In theory, therefore, a small brake pad will exert as much braking force as a large one of greater surface area. (12)
Although in theory a small brake pad will exert as much braking force as a large one of greater surface area, in practice a small pad will wear down more quickly and therefore is not used. (12+13)
However, in practice a small pad will wear down more quickly and therefore is not used. (13)
Similarly if we halve the mass carried, sliding friction is also halved. (17)
We can conclude that sliding friction is proportional to the reaction between the surfaces in contact. (18)

II

A 2. A force is set up which opposes motion.
3. Sliding friction between the two surfaces is doubled.
4. Sliding friction (between the surfaces) is reduced.
5. Sliding friction is reduced.
6. We find that the force required to start the block moving is greater than the force required to keep the block moving.
7. We find that the force required to keep the block moving is unchanged.
8. We find that the force required to keep the block moving is doubled.
9. We find that the force required to keep the block moving is reduced.

B 1. If we place a smooth roller on an inclined plane, the roller rolls down the plane.
2. When a table is pushed across a rough floor, a force is set up which opposes motion.
3. If the force pressing two moving surfaces together is doubled, sliding friction between the two surfaces is (also) doubled.

4. Sliding friction is reduced when we lubricate two moving surfaces.
5. Sliding friction is reduced if the surface of a shaft rotating in a bearing is greased.
6. If we measure the force required to start the block moving and measure the force required to keep the block moving we find that the former is greater than the latter.
7. If the block is laid on side A and the force required to keep the block moving is measured, it is found that the force required to keep the block moving is unchanged.
8. If we add a 1 kg mass to the block and measure the force required to keep the block moving, we find that the force is increased.
9. When a glass sheet is substituted for the friction board and the force required to keep the block moving is measured, it is found that the force required to keep the block moving is reduced.

C NOTE: the numbers here refer to the observations from exercise B which can be placed in column 1.
1. observation 2   This shows that friction always opposes motion.
2. observation 4 or 5   This shows that friction can be reduced by lubrication.
3. observation 6   This shows that static friction is greater than sliding friction.
4. observation 9   This shows that the value of sliding friction depends on the nature of the surfaces which touch each other.
5. observation 7   This shows that sliding friction is independent of the area of surface in contact.
6. observation 8   This shows that sliding friction is proportional to the reaction between the surfaces in contact.

①D 1. Steels mixed with one or more metallic elements are known as alloy steels. (defining)
2. Tests applied to materials are of two kinds – tests to destruction and tests within the elastic limit. (defining)
3. The power developed by the generator revolving at 1,000 rev/min, is 20 kW. (defining)
4. A dockside crane, mounted on a set of rails, has a safe working load of 3×10^3 kg. (non-defining)
5. The distance travelled by a moving load is plotted on a graph against time taken. (defining)
6. These forces constitute a tensile stress, known as hoop stress, which acts around the circumference of the cylinder. (non-defining, defining)
7. The force exerted on the clamps was found to be 1,200 N. (defining)
8. Bridges, roof trusses and cranes are structures designed to resist forces. (defining)

①E 1. XY is a steel shaft carrying a 300 mm diameter eccentric gear. (defining)
2. A flywheel, *consisting* of a cast iron rim connected to a boss by spokes, has a diameter of 1·6 m. (non-defining, defining)
3. The driving belt, which transmits power to the pulleys, is 9 mm thick. (non-defining)
4. The towers, *weighing* a thousand tonnes each, support the main section of the bridge. (non-defining)
5. The tapping head has a spring clutch, which allows the tap to slip without breaking when the load becomes excessive. (non-defining)

6. Grooving tools, which cut slots or keyways, are made of high-speed steel. (non-defining)
7. The main shaft of the lathe drives the lubricant pump, which supplies cooling fluid at the tool cutting tip. (non-defining)
8. Bronze *containing* 0·8% phosphorus is called phosphor bronze. (defining)

①F 1. Grey cast iron is a soft close-grained cast iron with a relatively low melting point.
2. A diesel engine having a running speed of 75 to 200 rev/min is called a slow-speed diesel.
3. A dockside crane with a safe working load of 2,000 kg is mounted on a set of rails.
4. A milling machine having a swivelling table is known as a universal milling machine.

①G 1. It was a suddenly applied load.
2. They are perfectly matched forces.
3. It is a rigidly fixed bar.
4. It is an easily corroded material.
5. It is a recently developed surface treatment.
6. It is a heavily stressed crane hook.
7. It is an externally heated salt bath furnace.
8. It was a deliberately exerted force.
9. It is a plastically worked forging.
10. It is an automatically controlled tool drum.

III

A NOTE: Readings from the graph within 3 rev/min of the answers given should be regarded as correct.
1. For 20 mm drills a speed of 130 rev/min should be used.
2. For 25 mm drills a speed of 100 rev/min ought to be used.
3. For 50 mm drills a speed of 50 rev/min should be used.
4. For 12·5 mm drills a speed of 200 rev/min ought to be used.
5. For 30 mm drills a speed of 80 rev/min should be used.
6. For 15 mm drills a speed of 165 rev/min ought to be used.

B 1. The shaft limits for a ball bearing of 10 mm bore should be 10·003 mm and 9·995 mm.
2. The shaft limits for a ball bearing of 30 mm bore ought to be 30·005 mm and 29·997 mm.
3. The shaft limits for a ball bearing of 60 mm bore ought to be 60·013 mm and 60·000 mm for a lightly loaded shaft.
4. The shaft limits for a ball bearing of 110 mm bore should be 110·028 mm and 109·990 mm for a heavily loaded shaft.
5. The shaft limits for a ball bearing of 65 mm bore should be 65·018 mm and 64·997 mm for a heavily loaded shaft and 65·013 mm and 65·000 mm for a lightly loaded shaft.

UNIT 5

I

A 1. rotate (2), 2. make (2), 3. the fulcrum (5), 4. distance at right angles (7), 5. the turning effect of a force about a fulcrum (6), 6. raise (15), 7. classified (17).

B 1. (b), 2. (a), 3. (a), 4. (a), 5. (c), 6. (c).

C NOTE: other word orders may be acceptable.

This means that a force can make a body rotate around a point which is not in its line of action. (2)

Thus a force can make a body rotate around a point which is not in its line of action. (2)

For example, if we push against the handle side of a door it will turn on its hinge and open. (3)

Since by the principle of moments we can say that the man will just balance the load when effort × a = load × b, any increase in the effort will raise the load further and may eventually cause it to overbalance. (14+15)

It follows that any increase in the effort will raise the load further and may eventually cause it to overbalance. (15)

II

A

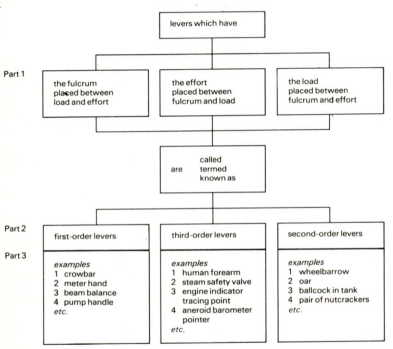

C Levers which have the fulcrum placed between load and effort are termed first-order levers. Meter hands and beam balances are examples of first-order levers.

Levers which have the load placed between fulcrum and effort are known as second-order levers. The wheelbarrow is an example of a second-order lever.

Levers which have the effort placed between fulcrum and load are called third-order levers. A steam safety valve and the human forearm are examples of third-order levers.

NOTE: This is not a complete list of all the paragraphs which can be made from the diagram.

D 2. A second-order lever may be used to move a large force with a smaller force.
A first-order lever may be used to apply a force remote from a point where an effort is made.
A first-order lever may be used to magnify a movement.
A first-order lever may be used to compare two masses.
A first-order lever may be used to move a large force with a smaller force.
A third-order lever may be used to modify the action of a large force by a smaller force.
A third-order lever may,be used to apply a force remote from a point where an effort is made.
A third-order lever may be used to magnify a movement.
3. A second-order lever may be used as a means of moving a large force with a smaller force.
A first-order lever may be used for applying a force remote from a point where an effort is made.
A first-order lever may be used as a means of magnifying a movement.
A first-order lever may be used for comparing two masses.
A first-order lever may be used as a means of moving a large force with a smaller force.
A third-order lever may be used for modifying the action of a large force by a smaller force.
A third-order lever may be used as a means of applying a force remote from a point where an effort is made.
A third-order lever may be used for magnifying a movement.
4. 1. A wheelbarrow is an example of a second-order lever used as a means of moving a large force with a smaller force.
2. A human forearm is an example of a third-order lever used for applying a force remote from a point where an effort is made.
3. An engine-indicator tracing point is an example of a third-order lever used to magnify a movement.
4. A steam safety valve is an example of a third-order lever used as a means of modifying the action of a larger force by means of a smaller force.
5. A crowbar is an example of a first-order lever used for moving a large force with a smaller force.
6. A meter hand is an example of a first-order lever used to magnify a movement.
7. A pump handle is an example of a first-order lever used as a means of moving a large force with a smaller force.
8. A beam balance is an example of a first-order lever used to compare two masses.
9. An aneroid barometer pointer is an example of a third-order lever used as a means of magnifying a movement.

①E 1. A chain drive is similar to a belt drive except that the chain passes over sprockets on the chain wheel, this arrangement ensuring that no slip takes place.
2. When a resultant force acts on a body an acceleration is produced, its value depending on the mass of the body.
3. The length of the steel increases in proportion to the forces applied, its cross-sectional area being unchanged.
4. The screw-jack is a screw revolving in a fixed nut, the screw thread providing a means of converting circular motion to motion in a straight line.

5. Work done by a force can be represented by a work diagram in the form of a graph, the vertical axis representing the force and the horizontal axis the distance moved.

6. The wheelbarrow is an example of a second-order lever, the load being carried between the fulcrum and the effort.

7. When a force is applied to the edge of a door it will turn, the hinge forming a fulcrum for the door.

8. Pressure is measured in newtons per square metre, the word 'per' implying that the force in newtons is divided by the area in square metres.

9. A crowbar is a first-order lever, the fulcrum being the heel of the crowbar.

10. The human forearm is a lever, the effort being provided by the muscle joining the upper arm to the forearm.

F 1. The main bearing consists of steel shells lined with aluminium in which the shaft runs.

2. The point about which the body is free to rotate is called the fulcrum.

3. The piers on which the bridge rests resist the load by a reaction of 5,000 N each.

4. The points from which the one kilogramme masses are suspended are 600 mm apart.

5. The position of the arms of the lever will depend on the angle at which the forces are required to act.

6. The rope to which the lower block is attached passes over one pulley in the upper block.

7. The distance through which the effort moves is double the displacement of the load.

8. Since earliest times man has tried to devise methods by which a small effort can move a large load.

9. The efficiency of most machines rises quickly to reach a maximum value near those loads for which the machine is designed.

10. A gear box is a unit in which a compound gear train which can be altered by engaging different gears is housed.

①G A speed governor is used to govern (the) speed (of an engine).
A mass carrier is used to carry masses.
A casing liner is used to line casings.
A gas generator is used to generate gas.
An air heater is used to heat air.
An oil cooler is used to cool oil.
A pressure regulator is used to regulate pressure.
A steam condenser is used to condense steam.
A shock absorber is used to absorb shock.
A hardness tester is used to test hardness.

a speed reducer   an oil-level indicator   a surface grinder
a fuel injector   an oil filter

III

High carbon steel contains between 0·55% and 1·20% carbon whereas medium carbon steel contains between 0·35 and 0·55% carbon. High carbon steel is stronger and harder than medium carbon steel, but its strength falls slightly when its carbon content is more than 0·83%. In addition, high carbon steel is less ductile than medium carbon steel. Medium carbon steel is used for railway rails, crank pins, connecting rods, axles, gears and gun barrels. High carbon steel with a carbon content up to 0·85% is used to make wood-cutting tools, locomotive tyres, crusher rolls, hammers and hand chisels. Car springs, tap drills and ball races are made from high carbon steel with between 0·85 and 1·05% carbon (content), while metal cutting and forming tools, drills and wire dies are made from high carbon steel with between 1·05 and 1·20% carbon (content).

IV

AIM   To investigate the turning effect of a force.

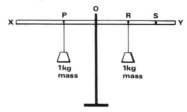

REPORT   A metre stick was pivoted at its centre point O so that it balanced. A cord was attached to a 1 kg mass and suspended from a point P on the side OX, 200 mm from the centre point. It was noted that the metre stick turned in an anti-clockwise direction.

A second mass of 1 kg was suspended from a point on the side OY. The distance between O and the mass was adjusted until the stick remained in a horizontal position. The distance between O and the second mass was measured and was found to be 200 mm.

The second 1 kg mass was replaced with a 0·5 kg mass. It was noted that the metre stick turned anti-clockwise. The 0·5 kg mass was moved along OY until the stick again balanced. The distance between O and the point S where the 0·5 kg mass was suspended was measured and was found to be 400 mm.

CONCLUSIONS   (i) The turning effect of a force depends on the magnitude of the force. (4)

(ii) The turning effect of a force depends on the perpendicular distance between its line of action and the point about which the body turns. (4)

UNIT 6

I

A 1. distortion (2), 2. the same c.s.a. throughout its length (9), 3. an elastic material (12), 4. extension (14), 5. extend (13), 6. exceed (20), 7. size and shape (11), 8. return to (11).

B 1. (b), 2. (b), 3. (a), 4. (a), 5. (b), 6. (b), 7. (a), 8. (a).

C NOTE: other word orders may be acceptable.

In more general terms, stress causes distortion. (2)

For example, a tensile force will lengthen a body. (7)

Whereas a tensile force will lengthen a body, one subjected to a compressive force will contract. (7+8)

In contrast one subjected to a compressive force will contract. (8)

For instance, if we take a bar of uniform c.s.a. of an elastic material like mild steel, . . . (13)

If we take a bar of uniform c.s.a. of an elastic material such as mild steel . . . (13)

In more general terms, strain is proportional to stress. (15)

For this reason, a graph of stress against strain would be a straight line . . . (16)

We can conclude that these findings illustrate Hooke's law . . . (21)

II

A A stainless steel is a steel which resists corrosion.
A non-ferrous metal is a metal which does not contain iron.
A formable metal is a metal which can be shaped into forms.
An abrasive substance is a substance which can be used to wear away a softer material.
A ferrous metal is a metal which contains iron.
A compressive force is a force which can shorten a body.
A ductile metal is a metal which can be drawn out into wires.
A tensile force is a force which can lengthen a body.

B If a steel is stainless, it resists corrosion.
If a metal is non-ferrous, it does not contain iron.
If a metal is formable, it can be shaped into forms.
If a substance is abrasive, it can be used to wear away softer materials.
If a metal is ferrous, it contains iron.
If a force is compressive, it can shorten a body.
If a metal is ductile, it can be drawn out into wires.
If a force is tensile, it can lengthen a body.

C If a material is elastic, it will regain its original dimensions after the forces which have caused deformation are removed.
If a material is plastic, it will not return to its original dimensions after the forces producing strain are removed.
If a material is tough, it will resist fracture when subjected to an impact load.
If a material is corrosion-resistant, it will resist corrosion.
If a material is rigid, it will not bend easily.
If a material is wear-resistant, it will resist wear.
If a material is brittle, it will tend to fracture under impact loads.
If a material is hard, it will resist abrasion, deformation and indentation.
If a material is soft, it will not fracture when indented or scratched.

①D a thin-walled metal tube   an indentor with four sides
   a flat-bottomed roller   a cutting tool with a stellite tip
   a six-sided poloygon   a hose with a wire jacket
   a multiple-edged cutting tool   a screw with a square thread
   a knife-edged follower   a rivet with a round head
   a cooper-faced rivet   a tool with a stub nose

①E 1. with   2. from   3. of   4. in   5. from   6. on   7. on   8. to   9. away   10. of (NOTE: 'of' is used when the object is composed of one material, 'from' is used when more than one material is used.)   11. between   12. with   13. to   14. into.

F 1. This shows that stress causes distortion.
2. This demonstrates that a body subjected to a compressive force will contract.
3. This shows that a tensile force will lengthen a body.
4. These findings show that strain is proportional to stress.
5. This demonstrates that a material which has the property of elasticity will return to its original size and shape when the forces producing strain are removed.
6. This shows that if we exceed the elastic limit, then strain is no longer proportional to stress and there is permanent deformation.

III

A 1. This graph shows that strain is proportional to stress.
2. These figures demonstrate that a body subjected to a compressive force will contract.

3. These figures demonstrate that a tensile force will lengthen a body.

4. These figures show that strain is proportional to stress.

5. These results demonstrate that if we exceed the elastic limit then strain is no longer proportional to stress.

B 2. Results 4, 5 and 6 show that if we compare the force required to cause movement with the force required to maintain movement, we find that the former is greater than the latter. This demonstrates that static friction is greater than sliding friction.

3. Results 2 and 3 show that the sliding friction force for wood on wood is greater than the sliding friction force for wood on glass. This demonstrates that friction between two surfaces depends on the nature of the surfaces in contact.

4. Results 1 and 2 show that if the area of surface in contact is halved, sliding friction force remains unchanged. This demonstrates that sliding friction is independent of the area of surface in contact.

5. Results 4 and 5 show that if the reaction between two surfaces in contact is doubled, the force required to cause movement and the force required to maintain movement are also doubled. This demonstrates that friction is directly proportional to the reaction between the surfaces in contact.

IV *The tensile test*

One of the most important mechanical tests is the tensile test to destruction in which a specimen is subjected to increasing tensile forces until it fractures. A specially prepared test-piece with a simple cross-sectional area, for example 100 mm², is normally used in this test. Such a test piece is illustrated in Diagram 1:

For a mild steel specimen a graph of load against extension for a tensile test may have the following appearance:

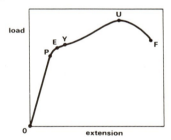

From O to P the specimen extends in proportion to the force applied to the material, thus illustrating Hooke's law. Soon after point P the material reaches its elastic limit, which is marked on the graph as point E. The specimen will regain its original length up to point E when the forces which cause tension are removed. However, if the elastic limit is exceeded the specimen will not regain its original length.

At Y, the yield point, the specimen suddenly increases in length for very little corresponding increase in force. After the yield point there is a rapid extension of the specimen with each increase in load until point U is reached. U represents the maximum load the specimen can undergo without change in its cross-sectional area. After the point of maximum load is reached, the specimen undergoes 'waisting'. This means that the cross-sectional area of the specimen narrows at some point in its length, as shown in Diagram 2.

Although the stress continues to increase, because of the decrease in cross-sectional area the load falls. The specimen lengthens further until point F when it finally fractures, as in Diagram 3.

UNIT 7

I

A 1. is known as (4), 2. required (9), 3. percentage (7) work against (7), 4. distance moved by the load (11), 5. has a fixed value (12), 6. the work input (14), 7. the work done by the machine on the load (15), 8. has no friction (21), 9. changes as the load it carries changes (6).

B 1. (b), 2. (c), 3. (b), 4. (a), 5. (d), 6. (a).

C NOTE: other word orders may be acceptable.
The M.A. of a practical machine changes as the load it carries changes since the percentage of effort required to overcome friction depends on the size of the load. (6)
For instance for very small loads a large percentage of the effort is needed to work against friction whereas with larger loads the fraction is less. (7)
For very small loads a large percentage of the effort is needed to work against friction, on the other hand with larger loads the fraction is less. (7)
Since some energy is lost inside the machine in overcoming friction, in practice the work output is always less than the work input. (17)
Hence the efficiency of a practical machine can never reach 100%. (18)
Because an ideal machine is frictionless, its M.A. would not vary with the load but would be a constant. (22)
Consequently a graph of load against effort would have the shape shown in Diagram 3. (23)
For this reason we could say that work input = work output. . . . (25)
An ideal machine would therefore have an efficiency of 1 or 100%. (26)
As efficiency is equal to the ratio M.A./V.R., the M.A. of an ideal machine must therefore equal its V.R. (27)

II

A 1. If we subject a steel bar to tensile forces, it will extend.
2. If we place a roller on a smooth inclined plane, it will roll down the plane.
3. If we apply an effort at E, the block will be raised/topple over.
4. If we subject a strut to compressive forces, it will (tend to) contract.
5. If we move the effort by 1 metre, the load will be raised by 1 metre.
6. If we attach a load to a spring balance, the spring will extend.
7. If we move the effort by 50 centimetres, the load will be raised by 25 centimetres.
8. If we move the effort by 1·80 metres, the load will be raised by 60 centimetres.
9. If we lubricate two bronze moving surfaces in contact, friction (between the surfaces) will be reduced.

10. If we replace the brass bushes in which a steel shaft is running with cast iron bushes, friction between shaft and bushes will be increased.

11. If we compare braking distances for a car on asphalt roads and on concrete roads, we will find that the braking distances on concrete roads are (slightly) shorter.

12. If we replace a leather belt driving a cast iron pulley with a plastic belt, the plastic belt will slip under heavy loads.

B 1. If we compared work output to work input for an ideal machine, we would find they were equal.

2. If we made a perfectly smooth surface, it would be frictionless.

3. If we measured the efficiency of an ideal machine, we would find it was 100%.

4. If we drew a graph of load against effort for an ideal machine, it would be a straight line passing through the origin.

5. If we prepared two perfectly smooth surfaces, they would have a zero coefficient of friction with each other.

6. If we calculated the M.A. of an ideal machine, it would be a constant.

7. If we compared the M.A. and the V.R. of an ideal machine, we would find they were equal.

8. If it required an effort of 10 N to raise a load of 100 N with an ideal machine, it would require an effort of 20 N to raise a load of 200 N.

①C 1. The 5 kg mass was removed to lighten the load on the test piece.

2. A reamer can be used to enlarge drill holes.

3. Repeatedly flexing copper wire hardens it and thus makes it easy to break.

4. A torque wrench should be used to tighten bolts on a cylinder head.

5. A tensile force will lengthen a body.

6. Wing nuts can be loosened easily by hand.

7. A compressive force will tend to shorten a body.

8. The surface should first be roughened using a coarse file.

9. Solvents can be used to soften coatings.

10. The gap between tailstock and spindle nose can be widened by rotating the hand wheel.

11. Friction between two rough planks can be lessened if they are planed.

12. Piston rings ensure that the piston makes a gas-tight seal with the cylinder wall.

13. Extra struts will strengthen the framework.

14. Dirty materials may weaken reinforced concrete.

III

A 1. The pulley wheel is to be made of die cast aluminium alloy.

2. The pulley wheel is to be 40 mm wide.

3. The end of the shaft is to be threaded M 20 for a minimum length of 25 mm.

4. The distance through the boss of the wheel must not be greater than 48·50 mm.

NOTE: The length of the bore in the diagram is 48 mm. The maximum size of the bore is 48+0·50 mm, i.e. 48·50 mm.

5. The diameter of the bore must not exceed 20·021 mm.

B The solid length of the spring must not exceed 2·600 cm.

The spring is to be cadmium plated to a minimum thickness of 0·0005 mm.

The spring is to have eleven coils.

The load the spring can support at working length 1 has to be not less than 13 kg.

The spring is to be stress relieved.

The wire size is to be 0·250 cm.

The outside diameter of the coil must not exceed 1·92 cm.

The spring is to be left-hand wound.
The inside diameter must not be less than 1·42 cm. (etc.)

IV *The screw-jack*

The wheel and axle, the lever, and the inclined plane are simple machines which man has used for over 2,000 years. Most machines are based on simple machines, for example the screw-jack is based on the inclined plane. Cut a right-angled triangle out of paper to represent an inclined plane, like that in Diagram 1. Wrap the paper triangle round a cylinder, such as the one shown in Diagram 2, so that the inclined edge of the paper makes a spiralling line round the cylinder, as Diagram 3 demonstrates. The spiralling line, which is known as a helix, becomes the thread of the screw.

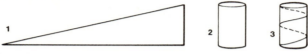

A screw with a square thread/a square-threaded screw forms the main component of the screw-jack. Square threads are used for power transmission because they offer less frictional resistance than vee-threads. The screw is free to rotate in a fixed nut which forms part of the body of the jack. The screw rotates, raising the load, when an effort is applied to the effort bar. When the screw make a full revolution the load is raised or lowered by a distance equal to the pitch of the screw. The pitch, which is shown in Diagram 4, is the distance between the same points on adjacent threads.

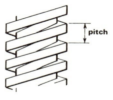

4

UNIT 8

I

PART 1 (a) feed pipe   (b) petrol   (c) fuel inlet   (d) needle valve   (e) float   (f) float chamber   (g) air   (h) jet of petrol   (i) throttle valve   (j) atomized fuel.
PART 2 cylinder head (11), induction manifold (12), cylinder (12), valve head (13), valve seat (13), valve stem (14), valve guide (14), valve spring (15), valve collars (16), cam (18), camshaft (18), push rod (20), rocker (20), tappet (22).
PART 3 inlet valve (25), carburettor (26), piston (27), sparking plug (28), cylinder (30), crankshaft (32), water jacket (33), exhaust manifold/exhaust valve (35).
diagrams   1. compression stroke   2. exhaust stroke
　　　　　3. induction stroke   4. power stroke

II

ΦA 1. The piston moves down the cylinder, creating a partial vacuum.
　2. The inlet valve opens, allowing the fuel mixture to enter the cylinder.
　3. The rocker tilts to the right, pushing the valve down.
　4. A poppet valve drops after two milliseconds, shutting off the fuel supply.
　5. The worm-gear revolves once, turning the wheel a distance equal to the lead of the worm.
　6. A tensile force is applied to the bar, stretching it by 0·09 mm.

7. The screw revolves once, raising the load by 30 mm.
8. The drum unwinds 100 metres in 20 seconds, lowering the pit-cage at a velocity of 5 m/s.
9. The brakes are applied when the car has a speed of 54 km/h, reducing its speed to 20 km/h.
10. As the governor spins, the weights pull outwards, raising the shaft collar and reducing the fuel supply to the engine.

①B NOTE: other solutions may be acceptable.
1. Gear B is rotated clockwise by rotating gear A anti-clockwise.
2. We lower the load by turning the effort bar in a clockwise direction.
3. To open the throttle, press the accelerator (pedal).
4. The bucket in the well is raised by turning the handle in an anti-clockwise direction.
5. We reverse the direction of rotation of pulley B by reversing the direction of pulley A/by crossing the pulley belt.
6. To apply the brake, pull the (brake) handle.
7. Gear B is rotated at 40 rev/min by rotating the motor/gear A at 80 rev/min.
8. We rotate gear B clockwise by rotating gear A clockwise.
9. To raise load L, apply an effort at E.
10. Gear B is rotated at 50 rev/min anti-clockwise by rotating gear A at 25 rev/min clockwise.

①C a seal which gas cannot pass through
a cement which is not damaged by oil
a grease which is not damaged by water
a coating which light cannot pass through
a connection which water cannot pass through
an engine cladding which sound cannot pass through
a surface which is not damaged by rust
a mounting which shock cannot pass through
a steel which is not damaged by corrosion
a surface which is not damaged by weather

III

1. a cylindrical piston   2. a T-shaped slot   3. a round rivet head
4. a square side plate with a circular hole in the middle
5. a semi-circular calliper gauge   6. a hexagonal nut
7. a triangular piston with curved sides   8. a V-shaped pulley belt
9. a kidney bean shaped combustion chamber   10. a conical spray
11. a V-shaped groove   12. a circular face plate   13. a conical point
14. a rectangular cross-section
15. an I-shaped cross-section (sometimes known as an I-beam)
16. a T-shaped cross-section (sometimes referred to as a T-beam)

IV *Pistons*
Pistons are cylindrical, cup-shaped steel or aluminium alloy castings. Aluminium is used because it is a good heat conductor and this helps the pistons to cool quickly. The closed upper end of the piston is called the crown. The walls of the piston, which are machined to fit the cylinder closely, are known as the skirt. The crown, which is normally flat but can be domed or dished, forms the lower part of the combustion chamber.
There are several grooves in the piston walls near the top and one groove near the bottom. These grooves are for piston rings which are circles of grey cast iron with a small gap in them. When they are unstressed they have a larger

diameter than the cylinder but when they are stressed they make a tight fit with the cylinder walls. They have two functions. The top rings keep gas from escaping from the combustion chamber and the bottom ring, called the oil-control ring, keeps the flow of oil which lubricates the rings and the piston to the minimum necessary. The bottom ring also clears surplus oil from the cylinder walls.

A hole through the piston holds the gudgeon pin which connects the piston and connecting rod. It should be hollow and of the floating type. The piston must be well-designed because it is subjected to compressive stress and must withstand both repeated impact loads and heat. In addition, in automobile engines it must move up and down at an average speed of 13 m/s.

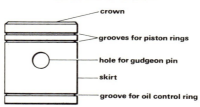

Key to questions on the free reading passages

NOTE: These answers should be regarded as a guide only and not as complete or model answers.

UNIT 1 *Corrosion*

1. Corrosion is any chemical action which affects materials in such a way as to damage their properties.
2. Corrosion increases the cost of a structure because regular maintenance, such as painting, is required to protect structures from corrosion.
3. Stainless steels are protected from corrosion by a thin surface layer of chromium oxide.
4. Monel metal is used for marine engine parts because it is resistant to corrosion caused by sea-water.
5. Cupronickels are alloys of copper and nickel which are resistant to fresh and salt-water corrosion.
6. Electrolytic corrosion occurs when two dissimilar metals touch each other in damp conditions. In these conditions a chemical action, like that occurring in a battery, is set up. This action corrodes one of the metals.
7. Corrosion can be controlled by using high-purity metals. Special corrosion-resistant metals like stainless steels or cupronickels can also be used. Alternatively surfaces can be coated, for example with paint, to produce a corrosion-proof layer.

UNIT 2 *Scales and Graphs*

1. A vector is used to give a pictorial representation of a vector quantity such as force.
2. A scalar quantity can be described by giving its size in a suitable unit of measurement.
3. A thermometer is a scale, graduated in degrees, for measuring temperature. The scale is read by noting the level of liquid in the thermometer.
4. Scales such as the metre stick can be used to measure scalar quantities. Scales like those employed in the slide-rule can be used to make mathematical calculations.

5. A slide-rule is two logarithmic scales used to make calculations such as multiplication and division.

6. A relationship between two variables can be shown by using a graph or a mathematical formula.

7. A graph gives an easily read pictorial representation of a relationship. A graph can serve as an information store.

8. A graph shows the relationship between two variables. A nomograph shows the relationship between more than two variables, and can be made in three dimensions.

UNIT 3 *Gravity*

1. Gravity is the earth's force of attraction on everything on or near its surface.

2. The weight of a body is the strength of the earth's force of attraction on the body.

3. Weightlessness occurs when the force of gravity is offset in some way, for example when the centrifugal force of a spacecraft in orbit round the earth offsets the earth's gravitational pull on the spacecraft.

4. Pens will not write in conditions of weightlessness because the ink is not attracted out of the pen by gravity.

5. People weigh less on the moon because the moon's force of gravity is less than that of the earth.

6. 9·81 is an approximate figure used in engineering calculations. The figure is in fact higher at the poles and less at the Equator.

UNIT 4 *Lubrication*

1. Friction between the screw and the body of the jack is so great that if the effort is removed the force the load exerts through the screw is unable to overcome friction. The jack cannot therefore run backwards. (Running backwards is known as overhauling.)

2. It is important that friction between a belt and a pulley wheel is high to prevent the belt slipping, especially when the pulley shaft is heavily loaded.

3. Friction reduces the efficiency of an engine because so much power is wasted in overcoming it.

4. The surfaces are not in fact perfectly flat. They are covered with tiny bumps. Welding takes place at the points where two sets of bumps meet.

5. Static friction is greater because an initial effort is needed to break the tiny welds between the surfaces before movement can take place.

6. Oil reduces friction because it forms a film between the surfaces and prevents them welding together and scraping against each other.

7. The oil itself hinders motion between the surfaces. The thicker the oil, the greater is the amount of power needed to start the surfaces moving over each other.

8. The speed at which the machinery will operate and the temperatures at which it will operate are important factors to consider when choosing a lubricant.

UNIT 5 *Beams*

1. A load will make a horizontal beam bend slightly. (This may not be detectable to the eye.) The top surface will be compressed and the bottom of the beam will be stretched. An excessive load will crush the top layers of the beam and tear the bottom layers thus causing the beam to fracture.

2. Tensile stress stretches a material.

3. The clockwise and anti-clockwise bending moments would each be 20,000 Nm. $(5,000 \times 4)$

4. Material at the centre of a beam undergoes very little compressive or tensile

stress when compared to the material at the outside of the beam. Most of the steel should therefore be concentrated on the flanges where the stress is greatest and not on the web.

5. A castellated girder is made by cutting a beam horizontally through the web into two pieces. The ends of the pieces are then reversed and the two pieces welded together again so that hexagonal spaces are left in the web.

6. The castellated girder is stronger than the original beam but has the same amount of steel in it.

7. The depth of the beam is important because it determines the magnitude of the beam's resisting moment to the bending moments which may destroy it.

UNIT 6 *Factor of safety*

1. Working stress is the greatest stress any part of a structure is subjected to.

2. The elastic limit of a material can be calculated from a tensile test.

3. Constant stress of one kind requires the lowest factor of safety.

4. Metal fatigue is caused by frequently repeated stresses.

5. Alternating stress varies both in size and direction. For example, it may vary from a maximum tensile stress through zero to a compressive stress equal in magnitude to the tensile stress. A connecting rod is subjected to alternating stress.

6. An engineer must consider the likelihood of overload and the conditions of service which may occur, for example the chance of a freak wind, when estimating the factor of ignorance.

7. The ignition of the fuel mixture imposes an impact, or suddenly applied, load on the connecting rod, hence a factor of 2 is allowed.

8. Aircraft are manufactured to low factors of safety because their weight must be kept as low as possible. Higher factors of safety would require more material in the plane's structure and would thus cut down their carrying capacity.

UNIT 7 *Cranes*

1. A hoist can only lift and lower a load whereas a crane can move loads in the vertical and horizontal planes.

2. Jib cranes have an arm from which the load is suspended.

3. An overhead travelling crane can move loads across the width of the load girder. Also, by moving the load girder along the gantry rails, loads can be moved parallel to the gantry rails.

4. A goliath crane is an overhead travelling crane with legs which run on ground rails rather than on gantry rails.

5. Shipyard cranes are used for the delicate manoeuvring of machinery such as engines when a ship is being fitted out. Such cranes must be able to place their loads with a high degree of accuracy, therefore fine control of the hook is necessary.

6. A kangaroo crane is a dockside crane which has a hopper at its base into which it feeds the cargoes it unloads.

7. Grabs are used for bulk cargoes such as coal which it would be impossible to handle with hooks.

8. A mobile crane either moves under its own power or is permanently fixed to a truck or railway wagon. A portable crane, however, must be moved under external power, for example by being pulled by a tractor or carried on a lorry.

UNIT 8 *The Wankel Engine*

1. The output shaft is connected to the piston by an eccentric gear linked to the inner bore of the piston.

2. The combustion chambers are formed between the walls of the cylinder and the sides of the piston.

3. When the fuel mixture ignites, the expanding gases subject the piston to a twisting moment which rotates it, thus compressing a fresh charge in one of the other combustion chambers.

4. The Wankel engine does not vibrate because its action is rotary and it has no reciprocating mechanisms.

5. The students' answers should include some of the following points. Those marked with a star are the most important points.

Wankel engine	*Conventional engine*
*The piston rotates round the cylinder following an elliptical path.	The piston moves up and down the cylinder.
The piston is triangular.	The piston is cylindrical.
The cylinder is roughly oval in cross-section.	The cylinder is circular in cross-section.
The engine has simple inlet and exhaust ports.	The engine requires valves to admit fuel and to allow exhaust gases to escape.
*The cycle of induction, compression, combustion and exhaust is carried out by the piston making one complete revolution in the cyclinder.	The cycle of induction, compression, combustion and exhaust is carried out by the piston making two up strokes and two down strokes in the cylinder.
*The rotary movement of the piston is transmitted to the output shaft through an eccentric gear and hence to the driving wheels.	The up and down movement of the piston must first be converted into a rotary movement before it can be transmitted to the driving wheels.
*The engine does not require a connecting rod and crankshaft.	The engine requires a connecting rod and crankshaft to convert the piston's reciprocating movement to a rotary movement.
The engine has little vibration.	The engine vibrates.
The engine is smaller and lighter than equivalent conventional power engines.	